THE ULTIMATE PEGAN DIET COOKBOOK

1000-Day Delicious and Environmentally Friendly Pegan Diet Recipes for Your Whole Family to Live and Eat Well Everyday. | 28-day Pegan Diet Program Included.

ALANA J. EILERS

Table of Contents

Introduction

When it comes to a healthy diet, we often find ourselves lost among so many options. Some common questions you might have are, Why are there so many types of diets? What is the basic difference between them? Which one is the best? Let's start at the beginning and start with what a diet is.

People often take diet as a synonym for weight loss, but that isn't the case. The Rock follows a diet consisting of 5-7 meals a day and weighs 118 kg, but he is still one of the fittest actors out there. The purpose of a diet is sound health and weight through the use of meal-specific nutrients for weight management and health reasons.

An example of a healthy diet is the Mediterranean diet which originates from locations surrounding the Mediterranean Sea. It has been found that the population in this area tends to have the longest life span.
Some diets focus less on what you eat and more on when you eat it. A popular form of this is intermittent fasting, which is used for weight loss, where you take all your calories in one go and fast for the rest of the day.

It is possible to combine diets to achieve your goal. Our "Pegan Diet" is made up of two words, "paleo" and "vegan" and has components of both diets.

What is a Pegan Diet?

The pegan diet was founded in 2015 and focuses on eating vegetables, fruits, and food that would be available to a caveman. This eliminates sodium, high sugar and carbohydrates. Vegan and paleo might seem opposite to each other and difficult to understand, but it's easy once you understand the vegan and paleo diets separately.

Paleo diet: Also known as the cavemen diet consisting of lean meat (less fat content), fish, and vegetables, its origin lies in hunting and harvesting.

Vegan diet: Free from all animal products like meat, fish, eggs, and dairy.

Pegan's diet follows Paleo's rule of eating wholesome food with minimal alteration by men and restricting certain dairy products.

Don't let the vegan confuse you
Before we move forward with the pegan diet, let us clarify one thing: the pegan diet is not a vegan diet even though it gets its name from vegan. In the pegan diet, you eat certain kinds of meat that are in their natural form and have a high content of good nutrients.

Benefits of the Pegan Diet
This diet provides a lot of health benefits that are not only limited to your ideal weight. These benefits cover mental health, skincare, and more energy. Let us take an in-depth look into the benefits of this diet.

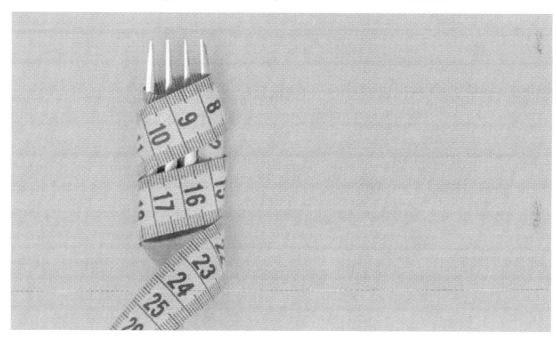

WEIGHT LOSS

Excess carbohydrates and sugar quickly get stored in your body as fat, so they can be used when you work out and move your body. Unfortunately, the amount of fat stored this way is often more than you need.
Good fats, a prominent part of the pegan diet, are not stored as fat because they are not processed by the liver and hence are used by your body for energy and different metabolic processes.
With a pegan diet that focuses more on what and when you eat instead of how much you eat, you can lose those extra pounds you have been trying to get rid of.

BYE BELLY-FAT

Unhealthy eating habits can lead to chronic inflammation and fat accumulation around your vital organs, which can increase your waistline. This chronic inflammation is also responsible for spikes in the level of cortisol which can ultimately lead to hormonal distress. A pegan diet can help fight and avoid chronic inflammation, reducing your waistline and easing your anxiety.

TAKE BACK THE CONTROL

Do you find yourself unable to say no to your food cravings? Many of us have this habit, but very few of us know that we can break it in only 7 days. All you have to do is stick to pegan for 7 days and avoid your cravings.

Pegan is a healthy, wholesome diet that keeps you full. Next time you are faced with cravings, remind yourself of the 7-day rule and remember that processed foods like sugar and carbohydrates can cause lifelong issues like diabetes and cardiac problems.

MAINTAIN THE CIRCADIAN RHYTHM

Ever heard the quote, "There is a time for everything and everything is meant to happen in its time?" Scientists know of many biological clocks. Usually, a plant respires at night and photosynthesizes during the day, but if there is no light during the day, the plant will still keep to its normal schedule. The plant, just like your body, needs food at specific times and requires time to process the food. On average, it takes 6-8 hours for your food to get digested. With this fact, you must be wondering why you get hungry every two hours. The answer is: because of an unhealthy diet and no routine. If you start eating healthy food on time, you will see a positive shift in your appetite and overall health.

IMPROVE MENTAL FOCUS

Getting rid of sugar and carbohydrates helps the body to stay highly active without feeling sluggish and sleepy all the time plus. Good food will positively impact your body and mind. Recent studies have shown good fats help neurons and the brain to work better. If you won't do it for your body, maybe you will do it for your brain.

GOOD GUT IS A GOOD DIET

Studies have shown that an increase in bad bacteria and a decrease in good bacteria in the gut have a negative impact on your digestive tract and overall health. With so many pollutants, the overuse of medicines, and a bad diet, it is very important to keep your gut flora full of good bacteria. One of the ways to do this is through probiotics, which are abundant in the foods that make up the Pegan diet, like vegetables, fruits, dry fruits, etc.

Tip: You can supplement with probiotic pills as well

IMPROVE GOOD CHOLESTEROL

You might see your overall cholesterol increasing after shifting to the pegan diet but hold your horses; it is because the pegan diet increases good cholesterol, and the bad one stays the same or goes down.

FINE-TUNE YOUR PALATE

Try cutting down on sugar for a week and then have something sweet and you will see and feel the excess sweetness that was otherwise part of your lifestyle; the same goes for salt. With a pegan diet, you can improve your palate, and you can do so by adding lemon to your food or extra garlic or onion, the perfect anti-oxidant ingredients.

HEALTHY SKIN

Many people consider their skin to be their body's most delicate layer. People tend to take good care of their skin since skin is the body's primary protection against harmful elements such as temperature, chemicals and bacteria. Additionally, your skin helps you stay cool during summer and warm during winter. In addition, your skin helps you keep clean by protecting your internal organs from harmful substances. Because of this, it's important to take good care of your skin.

Taking good care of your skin requires regular cleaning and proper food selection- but it's worth the effort!, eating antioxidant-rich raw fruits and vegetables will help you stay hydrated and reduce inflammation in your skin. These foods also contain essential vitamins and minerals that help maintain healthy hair, nails and bones. Along with a good diet, vitamins A and C supplements can also significantly improve the appearance of your skin.

The Pegan Syllabus

Let's talk about Pegan food and take an in-depth look at all the food you can eat in the pegan diet and their health benefits.

MUNCH THE PLANTS

Plant-based diets have been shown to improve the health of people from all walks of life.

A plant-based diet includes a variety of vegetables, fruits, nuts, seeds, and whole grains. Plant-based diets are also low in fat and sodium. Plant-based diets can help prevent chronic diseases, including cancer, heart disease, and diabetes.

Why do you need to be eating more plants?

Plants are full of fiber, antioxidants, and phytochemicals that reduce inflammation in the body. They also help cleanse your colon by removing waste material from your digestive system. Eating more plants will help you feel fuller for longer, so you don't feel hungry or want to snack on junk food! Plants also contain many vitamins and minerals that are essential for health, such as iron, calcium, potassium, and magnesium, which help maintain good bone density throughout our lives! Many studies have shown that those who eat more fruits and vegetables have lower rates of heart disease than those who don't eat them at all.

KEEP YOUR DIET CLEAN

There are numerous benefits of eating clean, healthy food. Not only does it provide the nutrients our bodies need to function properly, but it can also help us to maintain a healthy weight, have more energy, and avoid diseases.

There are many sources of clean, healthy food, including fruits and vegetables, lean meats, and whole grains. When we eat these foods, we get the fiber, vitamins, and minerals our bodies need.

Why eat clean? There are several reasons. The first one is a healthy weight. Eating clean foods helps us to do this by providing our bodies with the nutrients it needs without all of the empty calories. Second, eating clean helps us to have more energy. When we eat foods that are high in nutrients, our bodies can function at their best. Finally, eating clean can help us to avoid diseases. When we eat foods that are high in nutrients, we are less likely to get sick.

EAT ORGANIC

Organic food is produced by methods according to the standards of organic farming. Standards vary worldwide, but organic farming generally features practices that strive to recycle resources, promote ecological balance, and conserve biodiversity. Organizations producing organic products may restrict the use of certain pesticides and fertilizers in farming. Generally, organic foods are also usually not processed using irradiation, industrial solvents, or synthetic food additives. Currently, evidence in scientific and medical literature is insufficient to support claims that organic food is safer or healthier to eat than conventionally grown food.

OPEN THE DOOR FOR GOOD FATS

Eating good fats is a great way to improve your health and wellness.

Good fat sources include avocado, peanut butter, nuts, seeds, olive oil, and coconut oil. You can also eat these foods in moderation, and they won't negatively affect your health.

Some people are worried about eating good fats because they don't understand their benefits. Good fats are essential for good health and overall wellness. They include the following:

1) Monounsaturated Fats: These contain omega-3 fatty acids, which have many health benefits, including lowering cholesterol levels and reducing inflammation in the body.

2) Polyunsaturated Fats: These are found in plant-based oils such as sunflower or safflower oil. They help lower cholesterol levels by improving blood vessel function as well as helping to boost immune system function through their antioxidant properties.

3) Saturated Fats: These contain no cholesterol and can be found in meats such as beef, lamb, and pork, along with dairy products like cheese, butter, or yogurt, which are also high in calcium!

AVOID SUGAR

Many people know that consuming too much sugar can lead to health issues such as diabetes and obesity. Additionally, eating too much sugar can cause teeth decay and promote inflammation in the body. The health effects of sugar are well known. That's why most countries regulate the amount of sugar they allow in food products. Even so, sugars are still consumed in large amounts worldwide. Sugar is added to most processed foods as a sweetener- making those foods more appealing to consumers. Unfortunately, this has led to an obesity epidemic and numerous health problems associated with consuming too much sugar.

Eating processed sugar can cause cravings for more sweets and make you feel sluggish and depressed.

Research shows that people who eat more processed sugar are at higher risk for developing mood disorders like depression and anxiety, as well as eating disorders like bulimia.
The pegan diet contains natural sweetener alternatives to processed sugar.

Chapter 2
Begin a New Journey of Pegan Diet

The pegan diet is a hybrid of the paleo and vegan diet plans, combining the health benefits of both approaches. The main focus is on whole, real foods that maximize nutrition without consuming processed or refined carbs.

A healthy diet can decrease the risk of chronic disease and increase longevity. Eating a healthy diet is important for everyone, but it's even more important for people with diabetes and those who are at higher risk for heart disease, stroke, obesity, and other health issues.
Daily exercise and a healthy diet are not only great for your health but also for your mood and productivity. Exercise makes you more focused, has greater endurance, and improves your mood.

Some Pegan Ingredients

Meat and Poultry	Sea Food	Homegrown	Spices
Grass-fed Beef	Cod	Apple	Garlic Powder
Grass-fed Butter	Clams	Avocado	Onion powder
Organic Chicken	Lobster	Beets	Cumin
Organic Eggs	Mussels	Bell-peppers	Curry Powder
Lamb	Oyster	Carrots	Paprika
Turkey	Salmon	Garlic, Ginger	Oregano

Pegan-Approved Beverages

Studies have shown clear liquids have less sugar and less impact on overall blood sugar. Tequila has been shown to have the lowest impact on blood sugar and is lower in calories. Next time you get a drink, avoid sweet and heavy-calorie drinks and opt for the ones with no color or added sugar.

Some of the pegan-friendly drinks:
Water with lemon or lime.
Homemade nut milk.
Coffee with no added sugar.

Food to Avoid in Pegan Diet

LEGUMES

Legumes are a good source of protein, but if eaten in large quantities, they can slow down the process of digestion plus, they have starch and carbohydrates that convert into sugar. Pegan diet experts recommend eating legumes not more than ½ cup per day. But this does not apply to naturally and sustainably grown peas and beans, which are both tasty and beneficial.

DAIRY PRODUCTS

Cows in the US are fed hormones so they can be milked several times a day. When consumed, these hormones can spike cortisol, allergies, and bad skin. Yogurt is a good choice as it contains probiotics,

but make sure you eat it in a moderate amount and that it is made with grass-fed milk only.
Sheep and goat milk can be consumed as they are naturally pastured animals, so to be safe, choose them over cow milk.

VEGETABLES WITH STARCH

The pegan diet promotes vegetables, but it also asks to minimize the ones with high levels of starch as that can cause the sugar level to spike. This includes all types of potatoes, except purple or sweet potatoes and corn.

Active Life-Style is a Bonus

Healthy diet, healthy food, and healthy living. These are all words used to describe a balanced lifestyle that includes eating right, exercising, and getting plenty of sleep. They are often used interchangeably, but they are not the same thing. A nutritious diet is just that – a diet that consists of healthy food that gives you the nutrients you need to live a long, healthy life. A healthy diet can be enjoyed by anyone, and it can be adjusted to your taste preferences, health condition, and lifestyle.

There are many benefits to eating a healthy diet and exercising, from your weight and health, to how you look and feel. More specifically, being physically active can help prevent heart disease and some cancers, help you maintain a healthy weight, and reduce the risk of osteoporosis and type 2 diabetes. Exercise can even help reduce the symptoms of depression and anxiety. The NHS says that most people should do at least 150 minutes of moderate or 75 minutes of vigorous physical activity every week.

Chapter 3
4-Week Pegan Meal Plan

This is a 4-week pegan meal plan that will not only help you change your lifestyle but also give you some easy-meal ideas and in-depth knowledge about pegan food. By the end of the 4th week, you will see the difference in your health and everyday life.

Week 1

For the 1st week, we will go easy and keep it basic by using pegan-friendly ingredients that are already available at home. We will use less salt and gradually move to low-sodium food. For the first week, we will make at least two meals completely pegan-friendly and avoid processed and junk foods as much as we can. For this week's recipes, you will need some basic ingredients like eggs, avocados, and pastured chicken.

Meal Plan	Breakfast	Lunch	Dinner	Snack
Day-1	Grain -Free Nutty Granola	BBQ Chicken & Vegetables Sheet Pan	Red Lentils Curry	Mushroom and Quinoa Cups
Day-2	Overnight Chia Seed Pudding	Lamb Burger	Spicy Winter Farro Soup	Mushroom and Quinoa Cups
Day-3	Easy Avocado-Baked Eggs	Italian Baked Beans	Chicken Scarpariello	Cinnamon and Coconut Porridge
Day-4	Zucchini and Scallion Pancakes	Crispy Fried Sardines	Basil Parmesan Pork Roast	Banana Steel Oats
Day-5	Sweet Potato & Rosemary Waffles	Moroccan Pot Roast	Beef and Chili Mix	Quinoa and Cinnamon Bowl
Day-6	Veggie-Eggy Muffins	Rainbow Chickpea Salad	Vegetable Rice	Chickpea Snack Mix
Day-7	Veggie-Eggy Muffins	Beef Curry Stew	Orange Roasted Salmon	Chickpea Snack Mix

Week 2

For week 2, our goal is going to be no sugar and to adopt good things so you can reduce bad things. It is important to go zero-added and processed sugar for a pegan lifestyle. We will cook all three of our meals the pegan way and try out some delicious recipes. This week we will put our focus more on poultry and spices while keeping the low sodium mindset we adopted in week 1.

Meal Plan	Breakfast	Lunch	Dinner	Snack
Day-1	Light Ginger Tea	Grilled Chicken Taco Salad	Mushroom Burgers	Sweet Potato Pizza
Day-2	Apple Smoothie	Creamy Tuscan Chicken	Pegan Pancakes	Quinoa and Date Bowl
Day-3	Classic Switchel	Tomato Pork Chops	Chicken and Mustard Sauce	Beet Balls
Day-4	Baked Eggs in Tomatoes	Vegan Potato Pancakes	Strawberry Spinach Salad	Beet Balls
Day-5	Banana Milk	Chicken and Mint Sauce	Herbed Almond Turkey	Chia Seed Pudding
Day-6	Zucchini and Banana Bread	Broccoli with Lemon	Peas & Pancetta	Meatballs Platter
Day-7	Zucchini and Banana Bread	Simple Lemon Dal	Ritzy Veggie Chili	Meatballs Platter

Week 3

By the start of the third week, you are more than halfway through adopting a pegan lifestyle by eating low-sodium and sugar-free food and using organic ingredients. The third week involves fancy, high-end recipes that you may want to include in a dinner or lunch with friends. They are sure to be impressed by your cooking, and you may even convert them to a pegan lifestyle. This may be the point where unhealthy cravings are really kicking in but stay strong.

Meal Plan	Breakfast	Lunch	Dinner	Snack
Day-1	Sweet and Sour Juice	Thai Red Curry with Chicken & Zoodles	Israeli Eggplant, Chickpea, and Mint Sauté	Spinach Dip
Day-2	1-Pan Eggs with Tomatoes	Garlic Pork Tenderloin and Lemony Orzo	Slow Cooker Delicious Chicken Mole	Spinach Dip
Day-3	Golden Milk Creamy Smoothie	Sweet and Spicy Stir Fry with Chicken and Broccoli	Cannellini Bean Soup with Kale	Spinach Dip
Day-4	Cauliflower, Apple & Coconut Porridge	Slow Cooked Turkey and Brown Rice	Easy Beef Kofta	Tomatillo Salsa
Day-5	Coconut Strawberry Smoothie	Roasted Pork with Apple-Dijon Sauce	Yogurt Chicken and Red Onion Mix	Tomatillo Salsa
Day-6	Meat-Free Eggs Benedict with Lemon Sauce	Papaya, Jicama, and Peas Rice Bowl	Rich Bulgur Salad with Herbs	Arugula Pesto Couscous
Day-7	Mini Pegan Pancakes with Blueberry Syrup	Vietnamese Beef with Lettuce Wraps	Seafood Risotto	Arugula Pesto Couscous

Week 4

This week will mark the beginning of a new lifestyle in which you will eat healthily and stay healthy for the rest of your life. By the end of the fourth week, you will be thanking yourself that you chose this diet.

Let's get started with meal planning for the fourth week using all we have learned in the past 3 weeks.

Meal Plan	Breakfast	Lunch	Dinner	Snack
Day-1	Garlicky Zucchini with Poached Eggs	Pumpkin Moroccan Chicken	Pumpkin Moroccan Chicken	BBQ Jackfruit Pizza with Sweet Potato Crust
Day-2	Healthy Porridge	Gingery Chicken Lettuce Wraps	Curried Beef with Winter Vegetables	BBQ Jackfruit Pizza with Sweet Potato Crust
Day-3	Matcha Limeade	Flank Steak with Artichokes	Spanish-Style Saffron Rice with Black Beans	Muhammara Dip with a Twist
Day-4	Superfood Smoothie	Sea Bass Crusted with Moroccan Spices	Pistachio-Crusted Whitefish	Muhammara Dip with a Twist
Day-5	Fruit Infused Water	Lemony Turkey and Pine Nuts	Brussels Sprouts Hash	Crunchy Flax and Almond Crackers
Day-6	Hazelnut and Chocolate Milk	Tasty Grilled Lime Shrimp	Beef Steak with Shrimps	Mushroom Gravy
Day-7	Mixed Fruit Cocktail	Indonesian-Style Spicy Fried Tempeh Strips	Cauliflower Gnocchi	The Greatest Guacamole

Chapter 4
Breakfast Recipes

Grain-Free Nutty Granola

Prep time: 7 minutes| Cook time: 25 minutes| Serves 6

- 11/2 cups chopped raw walnuts or pecans
- 1 cup raw almonds, sliced
- 1/2 cup unsalted sunflower, sesame, or shelled pumpkin seeds, toasted or roasted
- 1/4 cup unsweetened coconut flakes
- 1/2 cup coconut oil or unsalted grass-fed butter, melted
- 1 tablespoon maple syrup
- 1 teaspoon alcohol-free vanilla extract
- 1 teaspoon ground cinnamon, or to taste
- 1/4 teaspoon sea salt or Himalayan salt

1. Preheat oven to 300F.
2. Set a rimmed baking sheet with parchment paper or foil.
3. Add the walnuts, almonds, seeds, and coconut flakes to a large bowl. In a separate bowl, mix the oil with the maple syrup, vanilla, cinnamon, and salt. Pour over the nut mixture, tossing to coat.
4. Scatter the mixture evenly on the prepared baking sheet and bake until golden brown, about 25 minutes, stirring once halfway through. Cool completely.

PER SERVING

Calories: 248 Fat: 25g Carbs: 6g Fiber: 3g Sugar: 2g Protein: 4g Sodium: 40mg

Overnight Chia Seed Pudding

Prep time: 5 minutes| Cook time: 0 minutes| Serves 1

- 3 tablespoons chia seeds
- 1 cup coconut milk or unsweetened nut milk
- 1 teaspoon alcohol-free vanilla extract
- 1 teaspoon maple syrup (optional)

1. In a large jar or bowl, merge all the ingredients, stirring to mix. Close or cover and refrigerate overnight.
2. The next day, add your preferred toppings and enjoy.

PER SERVING

Calories: 293 Fat: 19g Carbs: 21g Fiber: 17g Sugar: 1g Protein: 10g Sodium: 367mg

Mini Pegan Pancakes with Blueberry Syrup

Prep time: 5 minutes| Cook time: 15 minutes| Serves 4

- 1 very ripe banana
- 2 large eggs
- 1 tablespoon alcohol-free vanilla extract
- 1 teaspoon ground cinnamon
- Pinch sea salt or Himalayan salt
- 1/4 cup coconut oil, divided
- 2 cups fresh or frozen blueberries

1. In a medium bowl, press the banana until softened. Add the eggs and continue to mash until smooth and most of the chunks are blended. Stir in the vanilla, cinnamon, and salt.
2. Warmth 1 tablespoon of the coconut oil in a large skillet or flat cast iron pan over medium heat. Set in 2 to 3 tablespoons of the batter to form 3-inch rounds. Cook the pancakes four at a time until set and golden brown, 2 to 4 minutes total, flipping once. Transfer to a plate to cool. Repeat until the remaining batter is used up, adding 1 tablespoon coconut oil in between each batch.
3. In a separate, small saucepan, add the blueberries and remaining 1 tablespoon coconut oil. Cook over medium heat, constantly mashing berries with a wooden spoon, until juices reduce to a syrup-like consistency, 3 to 5 minutes. Set aside to cool.
4. Serve pancakes with the blueberry syrup on the side.

PER SERVING

Calories: 224 Fat: 17g Carbs: 18g Fiber: 3g Sugar: 12g Protein: 4g Sodium: 48mg

Easy Avocado Baked Eggs

Prep time: 5 minutes| Cook time: 15 minutes| Serves 4

- 2 medium or large avocados, halved and pitted
- 4 large eggs
- 1/4 teaspoon freshly ground black pepper

1. Preheat the oven to 425F.
2. Set out some of the pulp from the avocado halves, leaving enough space to fit an egg, reserving the pulp for Easy Guacamole (see the recipe Ceviche Fish Tacos with Easy Guacamole).
3. Line an 8-by-8-inch baking pan with foil. Place the avocado halves in the pan to fit snugly in a single layer, folding the foil around the outer avocados to prevent tipping.
4. Set 1 egg into each avocado half; season with pepper. Bake, uncovered, until the whites are set and the egg yolks are cooked to your desired doneness, 12 to 15 minutes. Detach from the oven and let rest for 5 minutes before serving.

PER SERVING

Calories: 433 Fat: 37g Carbs: 16g Fiber: 12g Sugar: 1g Protein: 16g Sodium: 154mg

Veggie Eggy Muffins

Prep time: 10 minutes| Cook time: 20 minutes| Serves 6

Extra-virgin olive oil, coconut oil, or clarified butter, for greasing (optional)
- 12 large eggs
- 2 teaspoons sea salt or Himalayan salt
- 2 teaspoons freshly ground black pepper
- 1 medium red bell pepper
- 1 medium orange, yellow, or green bell pepper, seeded and diced
- 1 cup packed baby spinach, finely chopped
- 1/2 cup thinly sliced scallions
- 1 small jalapeño pepper, seeded and minced (optional)

1. Preheat the oven to 350F. Grease a 12-hole muffin pan or use paper muffin liners.
2. In a large bowl, place the eggs, salt, and pepper and beat until fluffy. Add the peppers, spinach, scallions, and jalapeño, stirring to combine.
3. Ladle the egg mixture evenly into the prepared muffin pan.
4. Bake until a toothpick or paring knife comes out clean when inserted, about 20 minutes. Let the muffins cool before serving.

PER SERVING

Calories: 83 Fat: 5g Carbs: 3g Fiber: 1g Sugar: 1g Protein: 7g Sodium: 385mg

Meat-Free Eggs Benedict with Lemon Sauce

Prep time: 12 minutes| Cook time: 6 minutes| Serves 2

Hollandaise Sauce:
- 3 large egg yolks (save whites for other use)
- 1/2 cup extra-virgin olive oil, ghee, or clarified butter
- 1 tablespoon lemon juice (from about 1/2 lemon)
- Pinch salt
- Pinch cayenne pepper

Eggs:
- 2 teaspoons apple cider vinegar
- 4 large eggs
- 1 large ripe beefsteak or heirloom tomato, ends removed, cut into 4 thick slices
- 1 cup baby spinach
- Freshly ground black pepper

1. For the hollandaise sauce, bring a pot of water, filled to about 4 inches up the sides, to a boil. Set aside 2 tablespoons of the hot water. In a medium metal bowl, whisk the egg yolks. Add in the olive oil, hot water, lemon juice, salt, and cayenne and continue whisking.

2. However, the bowl over the pot of boiling water. Whisk constantly until the sauce thickens, 1 to 2 minutes, keeping the bowl from touching the boiling water, to prevent the eggs from curdling. Remove the bowl of hollandaise sauce from the pot of water, and set it aside on another part of the stovetop.
3. To poach the eggs, reduce the heat under the pot of boiling water to a simmer and add the vinegar. Prepare a paper-towel lined plate. One at a time, gently crack the eggs into a small bowl, and then use the bowl to slowly slide 2 of the eggs into the water. Simmer for 2 minutes. Using a slotted spoon, transfer the eggs to the paper towel-lined plate. Repeat the process with the remaining 2 eggs.
4. To serve, divide the tomato slices between two plates. Top each tomato with a few spinach leaves, 1 poached egg, and 2 heaping tablespoons of the warm hollandaise. Season with black pepper and serve immediately.

PER SERVING

Calories: 423 Fat: 39g Carbs: 6g Fiber: 2g Sugar: 4g Protein: 16g Sodium: 242mg

Zucchini and Scallion Pancakes

Prep time: 5 minutes| Cook time: 5 minutes| Serves 4

- 1/3 cup filtered water
- 2 tablespoons ground flax seeds
- 1 teaspoon coconut oil
- 3 large zucchinis, grated
- Salt and freshly ground black pepper, to flavor
- 1/4 cup scallion, chopped finely

1. In a bowl, mix together ground flax seeds and water and set aside.
2. In a large skillet, warmth oil on medium heat.
3. Attach zucchini and cook, stirring occasionally.
4. Set in salt and black pepper and immediately, detach from heat.
5. Set the zucchini into a large bowl and let it cool slightly.
6. Attach flax seed mixture and scallion and mix till well combined.
7. Warmth a griddle and grease it.
8. Add 1/4 of the zucchini mixture into preheated griddle.
9. Cook for 2-3 minutes. Carefully set the side and cook for 1-2 minutes further.
10. Repeat with the remaining mixture.

PER SERVING

Calories: 69 Fat: 2.7g Sodium: 27mg Carbs: 9.6g Fiber: 3.8g Sugar: 4.4g Protein: 3.7g

Garlicky Zucchini with Poached Eggs

Prep time: 10 minutes| Cook time: 10 minutes| Serves 2

- 1 tablespoon olive oil
- 2 small garlic cloves, minced
- 2 large zucchinis, spiralized with blade C
- Salt and freshly ground black pepper, to flavor
- 2 organic eggs

1. In a large skillet, armth oil on medium heat.
2. Attach garlic and sauté for about 1 minute.
3. Attach zucchini, salt and black pepper and cook for about 3-4 minutes.
4. Set the zucchini mixture into 2 large serving plates.
5. Meanwhile in a large pan, set 2-3-inches water to a simmer on high heat.
6. Carefully, crack the eggs in water one by one. Secure the pan and turn off the heat.
7. Keep, sealed for about 4 minutes or till desired cooking of the egg is reached.
8. Place the eggs over zucchini.
9. Whisk the eggs with salt and black pepper and serve.

PER SERVING

Calories: 179 Fat: 12g Sodium: 94mg Carbs: 12.2g Fiber: 3.6g Protein: 9.6g

Chia Seed Pudding

Prep time: 15 minutes| Cook time: 0 minutes| Serves 2

- 1 cup unsweetened almond milk
- 2 tablespoons maple syrup
- 1/4 cup chia seeds
- 1/4 teaspoon organic vanilla extract
- 1/2 of small apple, cored and sliced
- 2 tablespoons almonds, chopped
1. In a large bowl, merge all ingredients except apple and almonds and stir to combine well.
2. Cover and refrigerate for at least 30-40 minutes.
3. Top with apple and almonds and serve.

PER SERVING

Calories: 185 Fat: 9.8g Sodium: 92mg Carbs: 26.9g Fiber: 7.1g Sugar: 16.1g] Protein: 4.9g

Zucchini and Banana Bread

Prep time: 10 minutes| Cook time: 45 minutes| Serves 6

- 1/2 cup coconut flour
- 11/2 teaspoons baking soda
- Pinch of salt
- 1/4 cup coconut oil, softened
- 2 teaspoons vanilla extract
- 11/2 cups ripe bananas, peeled and mashed
- 1 cup zucchini, grated and squeezed
- 1 teaspoon orange zest, grated freshly

1. Preheat the oven to 350 degrees F.
2. Grease a loaf pan.
3. In a large bowl, merge together flour, baking soda and salt.
4. In another bowl, add oil and vanilla and beat well.
5. Add banana and beat till well combined.
6. Mix oil mixture into flour mixture.
7. Fold in zucchini and orange zest. Set the mixture into prepared loaf pan evenly.
8. Bake for about 40-45 minutes or till a toothpick nested in the center comes out clean.

PER SERVING

Calories: 166 Fat: 10.9g Sodium: 364mg Carbs: 15.5g Fiber: 5.2g Sugar: 5.8g Protein: 2.6g

Egg Breakfast Muffins

Prep time: 5 minutes| Cook time: 20 minutes| Serves 6

- 1 cup of diced broccoli
- Salt and pepper {to taste}
- 8 eggs
- 1 cup of diced onion
- 1 cup of diced mushrooms
1. Meanwhile, heat oven to 350 degrees F.
2. After which you dice all vegetables.
3. After that, in a large mixing bowl, set together eggs, salt, vegetables, and pepper.
4. Then pour mixture into a greased muffin pan, the mixture should evenly fill 8 muffin cups.
5. At this point, bake 18-20 minutes, or until a toothpick inserted in the middle comes out clean.
6. Finally, you serve and enjoy!

PER SERVING

Calories: 83 Fat: 5g Carbs: 3g Fiber: 1g Sugar: 1g

Sweet Potato & Bell Pepper Hash

Prep time:10 minutes | Cook time:17 minutes | Serves 4

- 1 tablespoon olive oil or edible coconut oil
- 1 medium onion, chopped
- 1 large sweet potato, peeled and cubed into ½-inch size
- 1 small green bell pepper, seeded and chopped
- 1 small red bell pepper, seeded and chopped
- Salt and freshly ground black pepper, to taste
- 2 tablespoons water
- ¼ cup scallion (green part), chopped
1. In a large skillet, heat oil on medium heat. Add onion and sauté for about 2 minutes.
2. Add sweet potato and cook, stirring occasionally for about 4-5 minutes.
3. Add bell peppers and cook for about 1 minute.
4. Add salt, black pepper and water and stir to combine.
5. Cover the skillet. Cook, stirring occasionally for about 10 minutes.
6. Stir in scallion and immediately remove from heat. Serve hot.

PER SERVING

Calories: 95Fat: 3.7gSodium: 20mg Carbohydrates: 14.6gFiber: 3g Sugar: 5.8gProtein: 1.7g

Sweet Potato & Rosemary Waffles

Prep time:10 minutes | Cook time:10 minutes | Serves 2

- 2 medium sweet potatoes, peeled, grated and squeezed finely
- 1½ teaspoons fresh rosemary, minced
- Salt and freshly ground black pepper, to taste

1. Preheat the waffle iron and lightly grease it.
2. In a large bowl, mix together all ingredients.
3. Place half of the sweet potato mixture in preheated waffle iron.
4. Cook for 8-10 minutes or till waffles become golden brown.
5. Repeat with the remaining mixture.

PER SERVING

Calories: 180Fat: 0.4gSodium: 14mg Carbohydrates: 42.4gFiber: 6.5g Sugar: 0.8g Protein: 2.3g

Blueberry & Pumpkin Muffins

Prep time:5 minutes | Cook time:18 minutes | Serves 5

- 2½ cups almond flour
- ¾ teaspoon baking soda
- ½ teaspoon ground cinnamon
- ¼ teaspoon salt
- 3 large organic eggs
- 1½ tablespoons pure maple syrup
- 2 tablespoons coconut oil, melted
- 1 teaspoon organic vanilla extract
- 1/3 cup homemade pumpkin puree
- 1 cup fresh blueberries

1. Preheat the oven to 350 degrees F.
2. Line 10 muffin cups with lightly, greased paper liners.
3. In a large bowl, mix together flour, baking soda, cinnamon and salt.
4. In another bowl, add eggs, maple syrup, coconut oil and vanilla extract and beat till well combined.
5. Stir in pumpkin puree and beat till well combined.
6. Add egg mixture into flour mixture and mix till well combined.
7. Gently, fold in fresh blueberries.
8. Divide the mixture into prepared muffin cups evenly.
9. Bake for about 14-18 minutes or till a toothpick inserted in the center comes out clean.

PER SERVING

Calories: 211Fat: 15.6gSodium: 354mg Carbohydrates: 10.1gFiber: 2.8g Sugar: 7.8g Protein: 7.2g

Baked Eggs in Tomatoes

Prep time: 25 minutes | Cook time: 20 minutes | Serves 4

- 8 tomatoes (medium)
- 2 tbsp. of olive oil
- 8 eggs (large)
- ¼ cup of Parmesan cheese, grated
- ¼ cup of milk
- 4 tbsp. of fresh herbs, chopped (like thyme, parsley, rosemary, or mixture)
- Salt & black pepper, freshly ground

1. Turn the oven on to 375°F. The olive oil should be used to grease a big oven-safe pan.
2. Cut the tomato stems off by cutting around them with a little paring knife. Scoop out the tomato's inside using a spoon. (Reserve the insides & incorporate them into salsa or tomato sauce.)
3. Place the tomato shells in the skillet as you have prepared them. Each tomato is filled with one egg. Add 1 tbsp. Milk and 1 tbsp. Parmesan over the top of each egg. Each egg should be salted and peppered.
4. Bake for 15 to 17 minutes, or until the whites of egg are set & the yolks are a bit runny, but the tomatoes are soft. After allowing it cool for five minutes, garnish with some fresh herbs. Serve right away.

PER SERVING

Total Calories: 288kcal, Fats: 19g, Carbohydrates: 12g, Protein: 18g, Fiber: 4g, Sodium: 100mg, Potassium: 55mg

Zucchini & Scallion Pancakes

Prep time:5 minutes | Cook time:5 minutes | Serves 4

- 1/3 cup filtered water
- 2 tablespoons ground flax seeds
- 1 teaspoon coconut oil
- 3 large zucchinis, grated
- Salt and freshly ground black pepper, to taste
- ¼ cup scallion, chopped finely

1. In a bowl, mix together ground flax seeds and water and set aside.
2. In a large skillet, heat oil on medium heat.
3. Add zucchini and cook, stirring occasionally for about 2-3 minutes.
4. Stir in salt and black pepper and immediately, remove from heat.
5. Transfer the zucchini into a large bowl and let it cool slightly.
6. Add flax seed mixture and scallion and mix till well combined.
7. Preheat a griddle and grease it.
8. Add ¼ of the zucchini mixture into preheated griddle.
9. Cook for 2-3 minutes. Carefully flip the side and cook for 1-2 minutes further.
10. Repeat with the remaining mixture.

PER SERVING

Calories: 69Fat: 2.7gSodium: 27mg Carbohydrates: 9.6gFiber: 3.8g Sugar: 4.4g Protein: 3.7g

Garlicky Zucchini with Poached Eggs

Prep time:10 minutes | Cook time:10 minutes | Serves 2

- 1 tablespoon olive oil
- 2 small garlic cloves, minced
- 2 large zucchinis, spiralized with blade C
- Salt and freshly ground black pepper, to taste
- 2 organic eggs

1. In a large skillet, heat oil on medium heat.
2. Add garlic and sauté for about 1 minute.
3. Add zucchini, salt and black pepper and cook for about 3-4 minutes.
4. Transfer the zucchini mixture into 2 large serving plates.
5. Meanwhile in a large pan, bring 2-3-inches water to a simmer on high heat.
6. Carefully, crack the eggs in water one by one. Cover the pan and turn off the heat.
7. Keep, covered for about 4 minutes or till desired cooking of the egg is reached..
8. Place the eggs over zucchini.
9. Sprinkle the eggs with salt and black pepper and serve.

PER SERVING

Calories: 179Fat: 12gSodium: 94mg Carbohydrates: 12.2gFiber: 3.6g Sugar: 6g Protein: 9.6g

chini & Banana Bread

Prep time:10 minutes | Cook time:45 minutes | Serves 6

- ½ cup coconut flour
- 1½ teaspoons baking soda
- Pinch of salt
- ¼ cup coconut oil, softened
- 2 teaspoons vanilla extract
- 1½ cups ripe bananas, peeled and mashed
- 1 cup zucchini, grated and squeezed
- 1 teaspoon orange zest, grated freshly

1. Preheat the oven to 350 degrees F.
2. Grease a loaf pan.
3. In a large bowl, mix together flour, baking soda and salt.
4. In another bowl, add oil and vanilla and beat well.
5. Add banana and beat till well combined.
6. Mix oil mixture into flour mixture.
7. Fold in zucchini and orange zest. Transfer the mixture into prepared loaf pan evenly.
8. Bake for about 40-45 minutes or till a toothpick nested in the center comes out clean.

PER SERVING

Calories: 166Fat: 10.9gSodium: 364mg Carbohydrates: 15.5gFiber: 5.2g Sugar: 5.8g Protein: 2.6g

1-Pan Eggs with Tomatoes

Prep time: 10 minutes | Cook time: 20 minutes | Serves 4

- 1 pint of cherry tomatoes
- 2 pounds of asparagus
- 4 eggs
- 2 tsp. of fresh thyme, chopped
- 2 tbsp. of olive oil
- Salt and black pepper to taste

1. Set the oven up to 400°F. Use nonstick cooking spray to grease a baking sheet.
2. Place the cherry tomatoes and asparagus in an equal layer onto the baking sheet. Olive oil should be drizzled over the veggies, which should then be taste-tested for salt, pepper, and thyme.
3. Roast in oven for 10 to 12 minutes, or until the tomatoes are crumpled, and the asparagus is almost soft.
4. Sprinkle salt and pepper on each egg before breaking it and placing it on the asparagus.
5. Return it into the oven & bake for a further 7 to 8 minutes, or until the whites of egg are set, but the egg yolks are still jiggly.
6. Asparagus, tomatoes, and eggs should be distributed among four dishes for serving.

PER SERVING

Total Calories: 158kcal, Fats: 11g, Carbohydrates: 13g, Protein: 11g, Fiber: 3g, Sodium: 200mg, Potassium: 20mg

Cauliflower, Apple & Coconut Porridge

Prep time:5 minutes | Cook time:20 minutes | Serves 6

- ½ cup cauliflower
- 2 cups apple, peeled, cored and shredded
- ½ cup coconut, shredded
- 1¾ cups fat-free coconut milk
- 1 teaspoon organic vanilla extract
- ½ cup banana, peeled and sliced
- ½ cup blueberries

1. In a large pan, add all ingredients except blueberries and mix.
2. Bring to gentle simmer on medium heat.
3. Reduce the heat to low. Simmer, stirring occasionally for about 15 to 20 minutes.
4. Serve warm with the topping of blueberries.

PER SERVING

Calories: 222Fat: 19gSodium: 28mg Carbohydrates: 13.7gFiber: 3.7g Sugar: 8.5g Protein: 2.4g

Healthy Porridge

Prep time: 5 minutes | Cook time: 15 minutes | Serves 2

- 2 tbsp. of shredded coconut, unsweetened
- 2-3 tbsp. of sunflower seeds, lightly toasted (or one tbsp. of tahini)
- 1 tbsp. of flaxseed or chia seeds
- 1 tsp. of ginger, ground
- 1/2 tsp. of cinnamon
- A pinch of turmeric, ground
- 1/2 cup of coconut milk or water, more if needed
- A pinch of sea salt
- 1 cup of chopped & cooked squash
- Some raw honey or pure maple syrup
- Extra toppings: cherries or berries, pomegranate seeds, coconut yogurt, or coconut cream to top.

1. In a blender or coffee grinder, combine all the dry ingredients (coconut chia, sunflower seeds, and spices) and process until the mixture resembles flour. If you're pressed for time, omit the sunflower seeds altogether and substitute tahini.
2. Add the mixture of dry ingredients to some coconut milk or water in a small dish, and let it absorb the liquid and gel up. You may save a little amount of gel for topping.
3. Blend the cooked squash & gel mixture until smooth in a blender.
4. The porridge should only be heated on the stovetop at medium heat until it begins to boil. Stirring every so while.
5. Remove from the heat, pour into your preferred bowl, and sprinkle the reserved dry mixture on top.
6. Add more milk, fresh berries, or other toppings.

PER SERVING

Total Calories: 331kcal, Fats: 17.7g, Carbohydrates: 43.1g, Protein: 7g, Fiber: 8.7g, Sodium: 180.4mg, Potassium: 50mg

Zoodles and Baked Eggs with Avocado

Prep time: 15 minutes | Cook time: 10 minutes | Serves 2

- 3 spiralized zucchini noodles
- Nonstick spray
- 2 tbsp. of olive oil
- 4 eggs (large)
- Kosher salt & black pepper (freshly ground)
- red pepper flakes, to garnish
- 2 halved avocados, thinly sliced
- fresh basil to garnish

1. Set the oven's temperature to 350 °F. Apply nonstick spray to a baking sheet to lightly oil it.
2. Combine the olive oil and zucchini noodles in a big bowl. Add salt and pepper to taste. Make each part into a nest on the baking sheet, then divide evenly into 4 sections.
3. Place a cracked egg in the middle of each nest. Bake for 9 - 11 minutes, or till the eggs are set.

Add red pepper flakes & basil as a garnish after seasoning with salt & pepper. Serve with slices of avocado.

4.
5. Per Serving
6. Total Calories: 633kcal, Fats: 53g, Carbohydrates: 27g, Protein: 20g, Fiber: 1g, Sodium: 15mg, Potassium: 210mg

Chapter 5
Juice & Smoothies

Mango Agua Fresca

Prep time: 5 minutes| Cook time: 0 minutes| Serves 2

- 2 fresh mangoes, diced
- 1(½) cups water
- 1 teaspoon fresh lime juice
- maple syrup to taste
- 2 cups ice
- 2 slices fresh lime for garnish
- 2 fresh mint sprigs for garnish

1. Put the mangoes, lime juice, maple syrup, and water to a blender. Process until creamy and smooth.
2. Divide the beverage into two glasses, then garnish each glass with ice, lime slice, and mint sprig before serving.

PER SERVING

Calories: 230 Fat: 1.3g Carbs: 57.7g Fiber: 5.4g Protein: 2.8g

Light Ginger Tea

Prep time: 5 minutes| Cook time: 10 to 15 minutes| Serves 2

- 1 small ginger knob, sliced into four 1-inch chunks
- 4 cups water
- Juice of 1 large lemon
- maple syrup to taste

1. Add the ginger knob and water in a saucepan, then simmer over medium heat for 10 to 15 minutes.
2. Turn off the heat, then mix in the lemon juice. Strain the liquid to remove the ginger, then fold in the maple syrup and serve.

PER SERVING

Calories: 32 Fat: 0.1g Carbs: 8.6g Fiber: 0.1g Protein: 0.1g

Classic Switchel

Prep time: 5 minutes| Cook time: 0 minutes| Serves 4

- 1-inch piece ginger, minced
- 2 tablespoons apple cider vinegar
- 2 tablespoons maple syrup
- 4 cups water
- ¼ teaspoon sea salt, optional

1. Combine all the ingredients in a glass. Stir to mix well.
2. Serve immediately or chill in the refrigerator for an hour before serving.

PER SERVING

Calories: 110 Fat: 0g Carbs: 28.0g Fiber: 0g Protein: 0g

Lime and Cucumber Electrolyte Drink

Prep time: 5 minutes| Cook time: 0 minutes| Serves 4

- ¼ cup chopped cucumber
- 1 tablespoon fresh lime juice
- 1 tablespoon apple cider vinegar
- 2 tablespoons maple syrup
- ¼ teaspoon sea salt, optional
- 4 cups water

Combine all the ingredients in a glass. Stir to mix well. Refrigerate overnight before serving.

PER SERVING

Calories: 114 Fat: 0.1g Carbs: 28.9g Fiber: 0.3g Protein: 0.3g

Easy and Fresh Mango Madness

Prep time: 5 minutes| Cook time: 0 minutes| Serves 4

- 1 cup chopped mango
- 1 cup chopped peach
- 1 banana
- 1 cup strawberries
- 1 carrot, peeled and chopped
- 1 cup water

1. Put all the ingredients to a food processor, then blitz until glossy and smooth.
2. Serve immediately or chill in the refrigerator for an hour before serving.

PER SERVING

Calories: 376 Fat: 22.0g Carbs: 19.0g Fiber: 14.0g Protein: 5.0g

Citrus Apple Smoothie

Prep time:10 minutes | Cook time:0 minutes | Serves 2

- 1½ cups chilled unsweetened almond milk
- 1 cup fresh baby spinach, chopped
- 1 cup fresh kale, trimmed and chopped
- 1 frozen banana, peeled and chopped
- ½ cup frozen pineapple chunks
- 2 teaspoons chia seeds
- 1 tablespoon matcha green tea powder

1. In a high speed blender, add all ingredients and pulse till smooth.
2. Transfer into 2 large serving glasses and serve immediately.

PER SERVING

Calories: 188 Fat: 3.8g Sodium: 163mg Carbohydrates: 40.6g Fiber: 6.2g Sugar: 25.6g
Protein: 3.6g

Simple Date Shake

Prep time: 10 minutes| Cook time: 0 minutes| Serves 2

- 5 Medjool dates, pitted, soaked in boiling water for 5 minutes
- ¾ cup unsweetened coconut milk
- 1 teaspoon vanilla extract
- ½ teaspoon fresh lemon juice
- ¼ teaspoon sea salt, optional
- 1(½) cups ice

1. Put all the ingredients to a food processor, then blitz until it has a milkshake and smooth texture. Serve immediately.

PER SERVING

Calories: 380 Fat: 21.6g Carbs: 50.3g Fiber: 6.0g Protein: 3.2g...

Apple Smoothie

Prep time:10 minutes | Cook time:0 minutes | Serves 2

- 1½ cups chilled filtered water
- 1 large apple, peeled, cored and chopped
- 1 large orange, peeled, seeded and sectioned
- ½ teaspoon lemon zest, grated freshly
- ½ tablespoon fresh lemon juice

1. In a high speed blender, add all ingredients and pulse till smooth.
2. Transfer into 2 large serving glasses and serve immediately.

PER SERVING

Calories: 102Fat: 0.3gSodium: 2mg Carbohydrates: 26.4gFiber: 5g Sugar: 20.3g
Protein: 1.2g ...

Beet and Clementine Protein Smoothie

Prep time: 10 minutes| Cook time: 0 minutes| Serves 3

- 1 small beet, peeled and chopped
- 1 clementine, peeled and broken into segments
- ½ ripe banana
- ½ cup raspberries
- 1 tablespoon chia seeds
- 2 tablespoons almond butter
- ¼ teaspoon vanilla extract
- 1 cup unsweetened almond milk
- 1/8 teaspoon fine sea salt, optional

1. Combine all the ingredients to a food processor, then pulse on high for 2 minutes or until glossy and creamy. Refrigerate for an hour and serve chilled.

PER SERVING

Calories: 526 Fat: 25.4g Carbs: 61.9g Fiber: 17.3g Protein: 20.6g...

Matcha Limeade

Prep time: 10 minutes| Cook time: 0 minutes| Serves 4

- 2 tablespoons matcha powder
- ¼ cup raw agave syrup
- 3 cups water, divided
- 1 cup fresh lime juice
- 3 tablespoons chia seeds

1. Lightly simmer the matcha, agave syrup, and 1 cup of water in a saucepan over medium heat. Keep stirring until no matcha lumps.
2. Pour the matcha mixture into a large glass, add the remaining ingredients, and mix well.
3. Refrigerate for at least an hour before serving.

PER SERVING

Calories: 15 Fat: 4.5g Carbs: 26.8g Fiber: 5.3g Protein: 3.7g

Tropical Fruit Smoothie

Prep time:10 minutes | Cook time:0 minutes | Serves 2

- 1½ cups chilled unsweetened almond milk
- ½ cup frozen pineapple chunks
- ½ cup papaya, peeled and chopped
- 1 frozen banana, peeled and sliced

1. In a high speed blender, add all ingredients and pulse till smooth.
2. Transfer into 2 large serving glasses and serve immediately.

PER SERVING

Calories: 151Fat: 3gSodium: 140mg Carbohydrates: 32.5gFiber: 3.6g Sugar: 23g
Protein: 1.8g ....

Fruity Breakfast Bowl

Prep time:5 minutes | Cook time:25 minutes | Serves 2

- 1 cup kiwi, sliced
- 1 cup fresh cherries, pitted and halved
- ½ cup fresh blueberries
- ½ cup fresh blackberries
- 1 tablespoon fresh lime juice
- 2 tablespoons maple syrup
- 2 tablespoons coconut cream
- ¼ cup pistachios, chopped

1. In a large bowl, mix together fruit, maple syrup and lime juice.
2. Divide fruit mixture in 2 bowls.
3. Top with coconut cream and garnish with pistachios before serving.

PER SERVING

Calories: 265Fat: 7.7gSodium: 19mg Carbohydrates: 48.3gFiber: 5.4g Sugar: 18g
Protein: 3.9g

Healthy Breakfast Bowl

Prep time:5 minutes | Cook time:5 minutes | Serves 4

- 2 cups unsweetened almond milk
- 2 large delicious red apples, peeled, cored and grated
- 3 tablespoons sunflower seeds
- ½ teaspoon organic vanilla extract
- ¼ teaspoon ground cinnamon
- 1 medium banana, peeled and sliced
- 3 tablespoons almonds, toasted and chopped

1. In a large pan, mix together almond milk, grated apples sunflower seeds, vanilla extract and cinnamon on medium-low heat.
2. Cook gently, stirring occasionally for about 3-4 minutes.
3. Remove from heat and transfer into serving bowls.
4. Let it cool slightly.
5. Top with banana slices and almonds.
6. Serve.

PER SERVING

Calories: 145Fat: 5.4gSodium: 92mg Carbohydrates: 24.7gFiber: 6.5g Sugar: 15.5g
Protein: 2.5g....

Fruit Infused Water

Prep time: 5 minutes| Cook time: 0 minutes| Serves 2

- 3 strawberries, sliced
- 5 mint leaves
- ½ of orange, sliced
- 2 cups of water

1. Divide fruits and mint between two glasses, pour in water, stir until just mixed, and refrigerate for 2 hours.
2. Serve straight away.

PER SERVING

Calories: 5.4 Fat: 0.1g Carbs: 1.3g Protein: 0.1g Fiber: 0.4g.

Superfood Smoothie

Prep time:10 minutes | Cook time:0 minutes | Serves 2

- 1½ cups chilled unsweetened almond milk
- 1 cup fresh baby spinach, chopped
- 1 cup fresh kale, trimmed and chopped
- 1 frozen banana, peeled and chopped
- ½ cup frozen pineapple chunks
- 2 teaspoons chia seeds
- 1 tablespoon matcha green tea powder

1. In a high speed blender, add all ingredients and pulse till smooth.
2. Transfer into 2 large serving glasses and serve immediately.

PER SERVING

Calories: 188Fat: 3.8gSodium: 163mg Carbohydrates: 40.6gFiber: 6.2g Sugar: 25.6g
Protein: 3.6g...

Hazelnut and Chocolate Milk

Prep time: 5 minutes| Cook time: 0 minutes| Serves 2

- 2 tablespoons cocoa powder
- 4 dates, pitted
- 1 cup hazelnuts
- 3 cups of water

1. Place all the ingredients in the order to a food processor or blender and then pulse for 2 to 3 minutes at high speed until smooth.
2. Pour the smoothie into two glasses and then serve.

PER SERVING

Calories: 120 Fat: 5g Carbs: 19g Protein: 2g Fiber: 1g...

Mixed Fruit Cocktail

Prep time:10 minutes | Cook time:0 minutes | Serves 2

- ¾ cup filtered water
- ½ cup fresh orange juice
- 1 teaspoon fresh lemon juice
- 1 teaspoon fresh lime juice
- ½ cup frozen mango, peeled, pitted and chopped
- 1 frozen banana, peeled and sliced
- 1 tablespoon shredded coconut
- 3 tablespoons coconut yogurt
- 1 teaspoon maple syrup
- ½ teaspoon organic vanilla extract
- 1 tablespoon coconut oil, melted

1. In a high speed blender, add all ingredients except coconut oil and process till smooth.
2. While the motor is running, slowly, add coconut oil and pulse till creamy.
3. Transfer into 2 large glasses and serve immediately.

PER SERVING

Calories: 184Fat: 8.1gSodium: 6mg Carbohydrates: 28.6gFiber: 2.5g Sugar: 18.6g Protein: 1.4g

Banana Milk

Prep time: 5 minutes| Cook time: 0 minutes| Serves 2

- 2 dates
- 2 medium bananas, peeled
- 1 teaspoon vanilla extract, unsweetened
- 1/2 cup ice
- 2 cups of water

1. Place all the ingredients in the order to a food processor or blender and then pulse for 2 to 3 minutes at high speed until smooth.
2. Pour the smoothie into two glasses and then serve.

PER SERVING

Calories: 79 Fat: 0g Carbs: 19.8g Protein: 0.8g Fiber: 6g...

Coconut Milk Peach Smoothie

Prep time: 10 minutes | Cook time: 0 minutes | Serves 3

- 1 cup of ice
- 1 cup of chilled coconut milk
- Some lemon zest
- 2 peaches (fresh) peeled & cut into chunks

1. To a Vitamix or blender, add peaches, ice, and coconut milk. Add some grated lemon zest to taste using a Microplane.
2. Blend until smooth at high speed.

PER SERVING

Total Calories: 187kcal, Fats: 16g, Carbohydrates: 12g, Protein: 2g, Fiber: 2g, Sodium: 10mg, Potassium: 356mg ..

Coconut Strawberry Smoothie

Prep time: 5 minutes | Cook time: 0 minutes | Serves 2

- 1 banana (frozen), sliced
- 1 cup of coconut milk
- 2 cups of strawberries (frozen)
- 1 scoop of collagen peptides (optional)
- 1 tsp. of vanilla extract

1. In the sequence specified, add each item to a high-speed blender.
2. Until smooth, blend.

PER SERVING

Total Calories: 346kcal, Fats: 24g, Carbohydrates: 27g, Protein: 8g, Fiber: 4g, Sodium: 40mg, Potassium: 680mg ...

Apple, Carrot, Celery, and Kale Juice

Prep time: 5 minutes| Cook time: 0 minutes| Serves 2

- 5 curly kale
- 2 green apples, cored, peeled, chopped
- 2 large stalks celery
- 4 large carrots, cored, peeled, chopped

1. Process all the ingredients in the order in a juicer or blender and then strain it into two glasses.
2. Serve straight away.

PER SERVING

Calories: 183 Fat: 2.5g Carbs: 46g Protein: 13g Fiber: 3g

Golden Milk Creamy Smoothie

Prep time: 5 minutes | Cook time: 0 minutes | Serves 1

- 1 cup of light almond milk or coconut milk (store-bought), use for creamier smoothie full-fat coconut)
- 1 cup of banana (ripe, frozen, and sliced)
- 1/2 tsp. of turmeric, ground
- 1 dash of ground cinnamon
- 1 tbsp. of ginger, fresh (plus some more to taste)
- 1 dash of black pepper
- 1 dash of cardamom and clove, ground
- 1 dash of ground nutmeg
- Optional:
- 1/4 cup of fresh carrot juice
- 1 tbsp. of hemp seeds

1. In a high-speed blender, combine the banana, turmeric, coconut milk, ginger, black pepper, cinnamon, and nutmeg. Blend on high until the mixture is creamy and smooth. If using, include clove, cardamom, & fresh carrot juice now (optional).
2. If it's too thick, add extra water or coconut milk. If too thin, add ice to thicken it.
3. Taste the food and make any necessary taste adjustments by adding extra cinnamon for the warmth, some black pepper for the spice, ginger for the zing, turmeric for earthiness or a deeper color, or banana for the sweetness. Carrot juice will intensify the orange/yellow color and add sweetness.
4. Enjoy immediately after dividing between serving glasses. Refrigerate any leftovers for 24 hours. Use any leftovers for future smoothies by freezing them by putting them onto an ice cube tray.

PER SERVING

Total Calories: 295kcal, Fats: 43.7g, Carbohydrates: 13.9g, Protein: 3.5g, Fiber: 4.6g, Sodium: 23.3mg, Potassium: 1104mg ...

Sweet and Sour Juice

Prep time: 5 minutes | Cook time: 0 minutes | Serves 2

- 2 medium apples, cored, peeled, chopped
- 2 large cucumbers, peeled
- 4 cups chopped grapefruit
- 1 cup mint

1. Process all the ingredients in the order in a juicer or blender and then strain it into two glasses.
2. Serve straight away.

PER SERVING

Calories: 90 Fat: 0g Carbs: 23g Protein: 0g Fiber: 9g...

Coconut Chocolate Smoothie

Prep time: 5 minutes | Cook time: 0 minutes | Serves 2

- 1 banana (frozen), sliced
- 1 cup of coconut milk
- 1 cup of ice
- 1 scoop of collagen peptides
- ¼ cup of cacao powder (raw)

1. In the sequence specified, add each item to a high-speed blender.
2. Until smooth, blend.

PER SERVING

Total Calories: 160kcal, Fats: 8g, Carbohydrates: 23g, Protein: 2g, Fiber: 5g, Sodium: 86mg, Potassium: 375mg

Chapter 6
Appetizers

Smoked Salmon Goat Cheese Endive Bites

Prep time: 15 minutes| Cook time: 0 minutes| Serves 4

- 1 package herbed goat cheese
- 3 endive heads
- 1 package smoked wild salmon

1. Pull the leaves apart from endives and cut the ends off of them. Add goat cheese to endive leaves. Add salmon slices on top of the goat cheese. Serve.

PER SERVING

Calories: 46 Carbs: 1g Fat: 3g Protein: 3g...

Baked tofu

Prep time: 10 minutes| Cook time: 10 minutes| Serves 4

- 250 g Japanese tofu
- 100 g of wheat flour
- 2 tablespoons oil
- 100g Daikon radish (Japanese radish)
- 1 piece of fresh ginger
- Japanese soy sauce

1. Dip the tofu briefly in cold water.
2. Drain, dab thoroughly and carefully cut into 8 equal cubes.
3. Turn the tofu pieces in flour and bake in hot oil in a pan on each side for about 1 minute over medium heat until golden brown.
4. Peel the radish and ginger and finely grate each separately. Squeeze out the radish and form four equal portions out of it by hand.
5. Arrange 2 pieces of tofu on each plate. Place a portion of radish next to each and decorate the top with ginger. Serve with a bowl of Japanese soy sauce.

PER SERVING

Calories: 149 Fat: 11.5g Carbs: 8.9g Protein: 2.4g...

Cheesy Cauliflower Frittata

Prep time: 10 minutes | Cook time: 30 minutes | Serves 4

- 2 tbsp. olive oil
- 1/2 lb. cauliflower florets
- 1/2 cup skimmed milk
- 6 eggs
- 1 red bell pepper, seeded and chopped
- 1/2 cup Fontina cheese, grated
- 1/2 tsp. red pepper
- 1/2 tsp. turmeric
- Salt and black pepper to taste

1. Preheat oven to 360 F. In a bowl, beat the eggs with milk. Add in Fontina cheese, red pepper, turmeric, salt, and pepper. Mix in red bell pepper. Warmth olive oil in a skillet and pours in the egg mixture; cook for 4-5 minutes. Set aside.
2. Blanch the cauliflower florets in a pot for 5 minutes until tender. Spread over the egg mixture. Set the skillet and bake for 15 minutes or until it is set and golden brown. Allow cooling before slicing. Serve sliced.

PER SERVING

Calories: 123 Fat 11 g Total Carbohydrate 7 gTotal Sugars 1 g Protein 14 g Potassium 245 mg...

Cilantro Mozzarella and Olive Cakes

Prep time: 10 minutes | Cook time: 25 minutes | Serves 6

- 1/4 cup black olives
- 1/2 cup low-fat milk
- 4 tbsp. coconut oil, softened
- 1 egg, beaten
- 1 cup corn flour
- 1 tsp. baking powder
- 3 sun-dried tomatoes, finely chopped
- 2 tbsp. fresh parsley, chopped
- 2 tbsp. fresh cilantro, chopped
- 1/4 tsp. kosher salt

1. Preheat oven to 360 F. In a bowl, whisk the egg with milk and coconut oil. In a separate bowl, mix the salt, corn flour, cilantro, and baking powder.
2. Combine the wet ingredients with the dry mixture. Stir in black olives, tomatoes and herbs. Set the mixture into greased ramekins and bake for around 18-20 minutes or until cooked and golden.

PER SERVING

Calories: 323 Fat: 11 g Carbs: 6 g Protein: 14.3 g...

Mushroom and Quinoa Cups

Prep time: 10 minutes | Cook time: 30 minutes | Serves 6

- 6 eggs
- 1 cup quinoa, cooked
- Salt and black pepper to taste
- 1 cup Gruyere cheese, grated
- 1 small yellow onion, chopped
- 1 cup mushrooms, sliced
- 1/2 cup green olives, chopped

1. Beat the eggs, salt, pepper, Gruyere cheese, onion, mushrooms, and green olives in a bowl.
2. Set into a silicone muffin tray and bake for 30 minutes at 360 F. Serve warm.

PER SERVING

Calories: 233 Fat 12 g Total Carbohydrate 4 g Total Sugars 2 g Protein 21 g Potassium 213 mg..

Zucchini and Mushroom Egg Cakes

Prep time: 10 minutes | Cook time: 15 minutes | Serves 4

- 1 onion, chopped
- 1 cup mushrooms, sliced
- 1 red bell pepper, chopped
- 1 zucchini, chopped
- Salt and black pepper to taste
- 8 eggs, whisked
- 1 tbsp. olive oil
- 2 tbsp. chives, chopped

1. Preheat the oven to 360 F. Warm the olive oil in a skillet over medium heat and sauté onion, zucchini, mushrooms, salt, and pepper for 5 minutes until tender. Distribute the mixture across muffin cups and top with the eggs.
2. Sprinkle with salt, pepper, and chives and bake for 10 minutes. Serve immediately.

PER SERVING

Calories: 245 Fat: 12 g Carbs: 2 g Protein: 12.8 g....

Cinnamon and Coconut Porridge

Prep time: 5 minutes | Cook time: 5 minutes | Serves 4

- 1 cup water
- 1/2 cup 36% low-fat cream
- 1/2 cup unsweetened dried coconut, shredded
- 1 tablespoon oat bran
- 1 tablespoon flaxseed meal
- 1/2 tablespoon almond butter
- 1 1/2 teaspoons stevia
- 1/2 teaspoon cinnamon
- Toppings, such as blueberries or banana slices

1. Add the ingredients to a small pot and mix well until fully incorporated. Transfer the pot to your stove over medium-low heat and bring the mix to a slow boil.
2. Stir well and remove from the heat. Divide the mixture into equal servings and let them sit for 10 minutes. Top with your desired toppings and enjoy!

PER SERVING

Calories: 276 Fat 21 Total Carbohydrate 3 gTotal Sugars 1.5g Protein 13.9g Potassium 342 mg...

Banana Steel Oats

Prep time: 10 minutes | Cook time: 10 minutes | Serves 3

- 1 small banana
- 1 cup almond milk
- 1/4 teaspoon cinnamon, ground
- 1/2 cup rolled oats
- 1 tablespoon honey

1. Take a saucepan and add half the banana, whisk in almond milk, ground cinnamon. Season with sunflower seeds.

2. Stir until the banana is mashed well, bring the mixture to a boil and stir in oats. Set heat to medium-low and simmer for 5-7 minutes until the oats are tender. Dice the remaining half of banana and put on the top of the oatmeal. Enjoy!

PER SERVING

Calories: 244 Fat 11 Total Carbohydrate 2 gTotal Sugars 2 g Protein 13 g..

Crunchy Flax and Almond Crackers

Prep time: 15 minutes | Cook time: 60 minutes | Serves 12

- 1/2 cup ground flaxseeds
- 1/2 cup almond flour
- 1 tablespoon coconut flour
- 2 tablespoons shelled hemp seeds
- 1/4 teaspoon sunflower seeds
- 1 egg white
- 2 tablespoons unsalted almond butter, melted

1. Warmth your oven to 300 degrees F. Line a baking sheet with parchment paper, keep it on the side. Add flax, almond, coconut flour, hemp seed, seeds to a bowl and mix. Add egg white and melted almond butter, mix until combined.
2. Set dough to a sheet of parchment paper and cover with another sheet of paper. Roll out dough. Cut into crackers and bake for 60 minutes. Let them cool and enjoy!

PER SERVING

Calories: 143 Fat 11 g Total Carbohydrate 3 g Total Sugars 1.7 g Protein 11 g...

Quinoa and Cinnamon Bowl

Prep time: 10 minutes | Cook time: 15 minutes | Serves 2

- 1 cup uncooked quinoa
- 11/2 cups water
- 1/2 teaspoon ground cinnamon
- 1/2 teaspoon sunflower seeds
- A drizzle of almond/coconut milk for serving

1. Rinse quinoa thoroughly underwater. Take a medium-sized saucepan and add quinoa, water, cinnamon, and seeds. Stir and place it over medium-high heat. Bring the mix to a boil. Set heat to low and simmer.
2. Once cooked, detach from the heat and let it cool. Serve with a drizzle of almond or coconut milk. Enjoy!

PER SERVING

Calories: 165 Fat: 9 g Carbs: 3 g Protein: 9 g...

Quinoa and Date Bowl

Prep time: 10 minutes | Cook time: 15 minutes | Serves 2

- 1 date, pitted and chopped finely
- 1/2 cup red quinoa, dried
- 1 cup unsweetened almond milk
- 1/8 teaspoon vanilla extract
- 1/4 cup fresh strawberries
- 1/8 teaspoon ground cinnamon

1. Take a pan and place it over low heat. Add quinoa, almond milk, cinnamon, vanilla, and cook for about 15 minutes, making sure to keep stirring from time to time.
2. Garnish with strawberries and enjoy!

PER SERVING

Calories: 323 Fat: 11 g Carbs: 6 g Protein: 14.3 g..

Chickpea Snack Mix

Prep time: 10 minutes | Cook time: 30 minutes | Serves 8

- 1 cup roasted chickpeas, drained
- 2 tablespoons coconut oil, melted
- 1/4 cup raw pumpkin seeds
- 1/4 cup raw pecan halves
- 1/3 cup dried cherries

1. Pat the chickpeas dry using paper towels. Drizzle coconut oil over the chickpeas.
2. Roast the chickpeas in the preheated oven at 380 degrees F for about 20 minutes, tossing them once or twice.
3. Toss your chickpeas with the pumpkin seeds and pecan halves. Continue baking until the nuts are fragrant about 8 minutes; let cool completely.
4. Add in the dried cherries and stir to combine. Bon appétit!

PER SERVING

Calories: 109 Fat: 7.9g; Carbs: 7.4g; Protein: 3.4g...

Sweet Potato Pizza

Prep time: 20 minutes | Cook time: 40 minutes | Serves 2

- 2/3 cup of rolled oats
- 1 sweet potato (medium), peeled
- 1 egg
- a pinch of garlic powder
- 1/2 tsp. of salt
- 1 tbsp. of olive oil

1. Preheat the oven up to 400 degrees. The sweet potato & oats should be processed in the food processor till very fine. Salt, garlic powder, and egg have been added. Pulse one more to combine. The ingredients ought to resemble a thick batter or loose dough.
2. Transfer to a circular pizza pan or baking sheet coated with parchment paper. You may either form two smaller crusts (you'll obtain more crispy side surface area) or one bigger crust by pressing into and shaping them with your hands. The ideal crust thickness is between 1/4 and 1/2 inch.
3. The top should feel dry when touched after baking for 25 to 30 minutes. Remove from the oven, let to cool, then flip back over onto the pan with dry side up. Olive oil should be brushed on after very carefully peeling the top layer off of paper. To obtain a lovely crispy top, bake for an additional 5 to 10 minutes.
4. Add your preferred pizza toppings, then reheat the pan in the oven to melt the cheese.

PER SERVING

Total Calories: 258kcal, Fats: 9.4g, Carbohydrates: 32.7g, Protein: 7.8g, Fiber: 4.8g, Sodium: 654.4mg, Potassium: 627.8mg...

BBQ Jackfruit Pizza with Sweet Potato Crust

Prep time: 15 minutes | Cook time: 15 minutes | Serves 8

- Pizza Crust:
- 1 pizza crust made with sweet potato
- BBQ Sauce:
- 1 tbsp. of tomato paste
- 1/2 cup of passata/tomato sauce
- 2 tbsp. of coconut sugar
- 1 tbsp. of apple cider vinegar
- 1 tbsp. of molasses
- 1 tbsp. of chili powder
- 1 tsp. of salt
- 1 tsp. of onion powder
- 1 tsp. of garlic powder
- 1/2 tsp. of mustard powder
- 3/4 tsp. of paprika
- 1 tbsp. of chipotle paste, optional
- Toppings:
- 1/4 cup of red onion, sliced
- 1 cup of jackfruit can, in water
- fresh cilantro

Get the crust (sweet potato) ready.
Jackfruit & BBQ sauce:

1. In a medium or small sauce saucepan, combine all the ingredients and cook them while whisking. Allow to boil for five minutes. Jackfruit should be rinsed and drained before being cut into smaller pieces. Here, you can mash everything together with a fork or a potato masher, but it is simpler to take apart bigger bits with your fingers.
2. The leftover BBQ sauce should be stirred into it before the jackfruit is cooked for a short time on low heat.
3. Pizza may be topped with red onions and jackfruit marinated in BBQ sauce. Bake for 10 minutes at 205°C/400°F.
4. Serve garnished with fresh cilantro!

PER SERVING

Total Calories: 146kcal, Fats: 1g, Carbohydrates: 25g, Protein: 2g, Fiber: 3g, Sodium: 589mg, Potassium: 250mg...

Muhammara Dip with a Twist

Prep time: 10 minutes | Cook time: 35 minutes | Serves 9

- 3 red bell peppers
- 5 tablespoons olive oil
- 2 garlic cloves, chopped
- 1 tomato, chopped
- 3/4 cup bread crumbs
- 2 tablespoons molasses
- 1 teaspoon ground cumin
- 1/4 sunflower seeds, toasted
- 1 Maras pepper, minced
- 2 tablespoons tahini
- Sea salt and red pepper, to taste

1. Set by preheating your oven to 400 degrees F.
2. Set the peppers on a parchment-lined baking pan. Bake for about 30 minutes; peel the peppers and transfer them to your food processor.
3. Meanwhile, heat 2 tablespoons of the olive oil in a frying pan over medium-high heat. Sauté the garlic and tomatoes for about 5 minutes or until they've softened.
4. Add the sautéed vegetables to your food processor. Attach in the remaining ingredients and process until creamy and smooth.
5. Bon appétit!

PER SERVING

Calories: 149 Fat: 11.5g Carbs: 8.9g Protein: 2.4g...

Spinach, Chickpea and Garlic Crostini

Prep time: 10 minutes | Cook time: 10 minutes | Serves 6

- 1 baguette, cut into slices
- 4 tablespoons extra-virgin olive oil
- Sea salt and red pepper, to season
- 3 garlic cloves, minced
- 1 cup boiled chickpeas, drained
- 2 cups spinach
- 1 tablespoon fresh lemon juice

1. Preheat your broiler.
2. Brush the slices of bread with 2 tablespoons of the olive oil and sprinkle with sea salt and red pepper. Place under the preheated broiler for about 2 minutes or until lightly toasted.
3. In a mixing bowl, thoroughly combine the garlic, chickpeas, spinach, lemon juice and the remaining 2 tablespoons of the olive oil.
4. Spoon the chickpea mixture onto each toast. Bon appétit!

PER SERVING

Calories: 242 Fat: 6.1g Carbs: 38.5g Protein: 8.9g..

Chapter 7
Poultry

BBQ Chicken & Vegetables Sheet Pan

Prep time: 45 minutes| Cook time: 50 minutes| Serves 4

- ⅓ cup of sugar-free BBQ sauce
- 1 teaspoon of salt
- 2 heads of broccoli, broken into florets
- 4 lemon slices
- Half tablespoon of oil
- chicken thighs, boneless & skinless
- 2 cups of russet potatoes, diced
- Half teaspoon of thyme
- 1 teaspoon of garlic powder

1. Coat the chicken thighs in BBQ sauce, mix well. Keep in the fridge for half an hour.
2. Let the oven preheat to 350 F.
3. Add potatoes to one side of the foil-lined baking sheet, toss with half the garlic powder and salt (half) and oil.
4. Oil spray the broccoli and add broccoli to one side of the pan and toss with the rest of the garlic and oil.
5. On one side of the same tray, place the chicken and brush with more BBQ sauce.
6. Bake for 40 to 50 minutes.
7. Serve.

PER SERVING

Calories: 378 Total fat: 14 g Total carbs: 6.9 g Fiber: 9 g Sugar: 4 g Protein: 32 g Sodium: 487 mg...

Creamy Tuscan Chicken

Prep time: 15 minutes| Cook time: 30 minutes| Serves 6

- 1 tablespoon of coconut oil
- 4 minced garlic cloves
- Sea salt & pepper
- 1/4 teaspoon of garlic powder
- 1 cup of chicken broth
- 1.5 lbs. of boneless & skinless chicken thighs
- 1/4 teaspoon of onion powder
- 1 chopped onion
- 1 tablespoon of tapioca flour
- 1 1/2 cups of chopped baby spinach
- Half cup of coconut milk
- Half tablespoon of ground mustard
- 1 1/2 tablespoon of nutritional yeast
- Salt & pepper, to taste
- 1 teaspoon of Italian seasoning blend
- 2/3 cup of chopped sun-dried tomatoes

1. Season the chicken with onion powder, salt, garlic and pepper.
2. In a skillet, add oil on medium heat. Cook chicken for 5 to 7 minutes on one side, take it out on a plate.
3. Add onions and cook until tender; add garlic and cook for 45 seconds.
4. Add tapioca and coconut milk, and broth. Whisk well.
5. Add Italian seasoning, mustard, salt, pepper and yeast. Cook till it starts to thicken.
6. Add tomatoes and spinach and cook until spinach wilts; add the chicken back in the pan.
7. Cook for 2 minutes, serve.

PER SERVING

Calories: 368 Total fat: 25 g Total carbs: 12 g Fiber: 2 g Sugar: 5 g Protein: 23 g Sodium: 253 mg..

Spicy and Sweet Chicken Stir Fry with Broccoli

Prep time: 10 minutes | Cook time: 20 minutes | Serves 4

- 1 tbsp. of olive oil
- 3 cups of broccoli florets
- 2 boneless & skinless halves of chicken breast, cut in 1-inch strips
- 4 cloves of garlic, thinly sliced
- ¼ cup of sliced green onions
- 1 tbsp. of hoisin sauce
- 1 tbsp. of low sodium soy sauce
- 1 tbsp. of chile paste
- ½ tsp. of ground ginger
- ½ tsp. of salt
- ¼ tsp. of crushed red pepper
- ⅛ cup of chicken stock
- ½ tsp. of black pepper

1. In a steamer with 1" of boiling water, add the broccoli and close the lid. Cook for approximately 5 minutes, or until fork-tender but firm.
2. Chicken, garlic, and green onions should be sautéed in oil over medium heat till the chicken is not pink anymore and the juices flow clear.
3. Add the ginger, salt, red pepper, and black pepper to the pan along with the hoisin sauce, chili paste, and soy sauce. Add the chicken stock & stir, then simmer for approximately two minutes. Add the steamed broccoli and combine until the broccoli is evenly covered.

PER SERVING

Total Calories: 156kcal, Fats: 6.2g, Carbohydrates: 10.9g, Protein: 15.9g, Fiber: 2.3g, Sodium: 606.4mg, Potassium: 379.1mg...

Oregano Turkey and Peppers

Prep time: 10 minutes | Cook time:1 hour | Serves 4

- 2 red bell peppers, cut into strips
- 2 green bell peppers, cut into strips
- 1 red onion, chopped
- 4 garlic cloves, minced
- ½ cup black olives, pitted and sliced
- 2 cups chicken stock
- 1 big turkey breast, skinless, boneless and cut into strips
- 1 tablespoon oregano, chopped
- ½ cup cilantro, chopped

1. In a baking pan, combine the peppers with the turkey and the rest of the ingredients, toss, place in the oven at 400 degrees F and roast for 1 hour.
2. Divide the meal between plates and serve.

PER SERVING

Calories: 229, Fat: 8.9, Fiber: 8.2, Carbs: 17.8, Protein: 33.6

Chicken & Mixed Vegetables Casserole

Prep time:10 minutes | Cook time:55 minutes | Serves 6

6 organic eggs
- 2 tablespoons fresh cilantro, minced
- ¼ teaspoon red pepper flakes, crushed
- Salt and freshly ground black pepper, to taste
- 1 cup fresh kale, trimmed and chopped
- 3 medium zucchinis, grated
- 1 cup fresh mushrooms, chopped
- 1 medium onion, chopped
- 1 cup cooked organic chicken, shredded
- 2 tablespoons almond flour

1. Preheat the oven to 400 degrees F.
2. Lightly, grease an 8x8-inch casserole dish.
3. In a medium bowl, add eggs, cilantro, red pepper flakes, salt and black pepper and beat till well combined. Keep aside.
4. In another large bowl, mix together all vegetables.
5. Transfer the vegetable mixture into prepared casserole dish evenly.
6. Place shredded chicken over vegetable mixture evenly.
7. Sprinkle with almond flour evenly.
8. Top with egg mixture evenly.
9. Bake for about 45-55 minutes or till top is golden brown.

PER SERVING

Calories: 141Fat: 6.3gSodium: 93mg Carbohydrates: 7.3gFiber: 2g Sugar: 3.1gProtein: 14.8g ..

Grilled Chicken Taco Salad

Prep time: 15 minutes | Cook time: 30 minutes| Serves 4

- 3/4-pound skinless, boneless chicken breast halves
- 3 (7 inch) corn tortillas
- 3 cups shredded lettuce
- 1/4 cup and 2 tablespoons chopped fresh cilantro
- 2-1/4 teaspoons lime juice
- 1 tablespoon and 1-1/2 teaspoons chili powder
- 3/4 teaspoon ground cumin
- 3/4 teaspoon ground coriander
- 1-1/4 teaspoons brown sugar
- 1/8 teaspoon cayenne pepper
- 2-1/4 teaspoons olive oil
- 3/4 avocado - peeled, pitted, and sliced (optional)
- 3/4 lime, cut into wedges (optional)
- 3 tablespoons sour cream (optional)

1. Preheat an outdoor grill for medium-high heat and lightly oil the grate.
2. In a bowl, mix black beans, salsa, 1/2 cup cilantro, and lime juice and set aside.
3. Stir chili powder, cumin, coriander, brown sugar, cayenne pepper, and olive oil in a bowl until smooth; rub mixture over chicken breasts.
4. Cook chicken breasts on preheated grill until no longer pink in the center and the juices run clear, 10 to 12 minutes per side. An instant-read thermometer inserted into the center should read at least 165 degrees F (74 degrees C).
5. Place tortillas on grill while Chicken is cooking and grill until lightly brown on both sides, 3 to 5 minutes.
6. Transfer chicken to a cutting board and slice into long thin strips. Divide chicken strips over tortillas and top with bean mixture, lettuce, and remaining 1/2 cup cilantro.
7. Serve with avocado, lime wedges, and sour cream.

PER SERVING

Calorie 470, Fats `18.7g, Carbs 44.4g, Protein 35.2g..

Chicken and Mint Sauce

Prep time: 10 minutes | Cook time:30 minutes | Serves 4

- 2 and ½ tablespoons olive oil
- 2 pounds chicken breasts, skinless, boneless and halved
- 3 tablespoons garlic, minced
- 2 tablespoons lemon juice
- 1 tablespoon red wine vinegar
- 1/3 cup Greek yogurt
- 2 tablespoons mint, chopped
- A pinch of salt and black pepper

1. Place the garlic plus lemon juice and the other ingredients except the oil and the chicken in a blender and pulse well.
2. Warm up a pan with the oil over medium-high heat, add the chicken and brown for 3 minutes on each side.
3. Add the mint sauce, place in the oven and bake everything at 370 degrees F for 25 minutes.
4. Divide the chicken mixture between plates and serve.

PER SERVING

Calories: 278, Fat; 12, Fiber: 11.2, Carbs: 18.1, Protein: 13.3

Chicken and Mustard Sauce

Prep time: 10 minutes | Cook time:26 minutes | Serves 4

- 1/3 cup mustard
- Salt and black pepper to the taste
- 1 red onion, chopped
- 1 tablespoon olive oil
- 1 and ½ cups chicken stock
- 4 chicken breasts, skinless, boneless, and halved
- ¼ teaspoon oregano, dried

1. Heat a pan with the stock over medium heat, add the mustard, onion, salt, pepper and the oregano, whisk, bring to a simmer and cook for 8 minutes.
2. Warm another pan with the oil over medium-high heat, add the chicken and brown for 3 minutes on both sides.
3. Add chicken into the pan with the sauce, mix well, simmer everything for 12 minutes more, divide between plates and serve.

PER SERVING

Calories: 247, Fat: 15.1, Fiber: 9.1, Carbs: 16.6, Protein: 26.1

Pumpkin Moroccan Chicken

Prep Time: 20 minutes | Cook time: 4 hours | Serves 8

- 1 tbsp. of olive oil
- 2 pounds of chicken breasts, in chunks
- 1 chopped onion
- 2 tsp. of cumin
- 2 tsp. of ginger powder
- 1 tsp. of sea salt
- 1/2 tsp. of turmeric
- 1 tsp. of cinnamon
- 1/4 tsp. of cayenne
- 1 cup of vegetable or chicken broth
- 1 cup of fresh pumpkin, canned also works
- toasted almonds, for garnishing, optional
- chopped cilantro to garnish

1. Add 1/2 tbsp. of olive oil to a frying pan on high heat. Sauté the onion till transparent after adding it.
2. Add the chicken pieces and heat until browned but not fully cooked.
3. Add salt & spices after the chicken has begun to brown, then stir to coat the chicken and onions in a uniform layer.
4. Pumpkin puree & vegetable broth should be added to the crockpot after the chicken & onions have been added. The pumpkin puree should be mixed into the chicken mixture while stirring.
5. For four hours, cook on low heat. This may also be cooked for two hours on high, but the texture won't be as excellent.

PER SERVING

Total Calories: 167kcal, Fat: 5g, Carbohydrates: 5g, Protein: 25g, Fiber: 1g, Sodium: 543mg, Potassium: 518mg

Sweet and Spicy Stir Fry with Chicken and Broccoli

Prep time: 5 minutes | Cook time: 10 minutes | Serves 3

- 1 tablespoon and 3/4 teaspoon low sodium soy sauce
- 1/2 teaspoon ground ginger
- 1/4 teaspoon crushed red pepper
- 1/2 teaspoon salt
- 3-3/4 cups and 2 tablespoons broccoli florets
- 1 tablespoon and 3/4 teaspoon olive oil
- 2-1/2 skinless, boneless chicken breast halves - cut into 1-inch strips
- 1/3 cup sliced green onions
- 5 cloves garlic, thinly sliced
- 1 tablespoon and 3/4 teaspoon hoisin sauce
- 1 tablespoon and 3/4 teaspoon chile paste
- 1/2 teaspoon black pepper
- 2 tablespoons and 1/2 teaspoon chicken stock

1. Place broccoli in a steamer over 1 inch of boiling water, and cover. Cook for about 5 minutes until tender but still firm.
2. In a skillet over medium heat, heat the oil and sauté the chicken, green onions, and garlic until

the chicken is no longer pink and juices run clear.
3. Stir the hoisin sauce, Chile paste, and soy sauce into the skillet; season with ginger, red pepper, salt, and black pepper. Stir in the chicken stock and simmer about 2 minutes.
4. Mix in the steamed broccoli until coated with the sauce mixture.

PER SERVING

Calorie 292, Fats `12g, Carbs 15g, Protein 34g..

Thai Red Curry with Chicken & Zoodles

Prep Time: 20 minutes | Cook time: 30 minutes | Serves 6

- 3 cloves of garlic minced
- 1 tbsp. of avocado oil or substitute olive oil
- 3 tbsp. of ginger, grated
- 2 cups of vegetable or chicken broth
- 1/2 tsp. of turmeric
- 1/4 cup of SunButter (No Added Sugar)
- 1 pound of chicken breasts, thinly sliced or cubed
- 2 tbsp. of paste of Thai red curry, add less if needed
- 1 sweet potato (large), peeled & cubed
- 1 red bell pepper, in thin strips
- 1 can of full-fat coconut milk (14 ounces)
- 1 cup of thinly sliced red onion
- 2 tbsp. of fresh lime juice
- 3 tbsp. of coconut aminos or 1 & 1/2 tbsp. of soy sauce or tamari
- 1 zucchini (large) zoodles, about 6 cups
- Some chopped green onions for garnishing, optional
- Chopped cilantro for garnishing, optional

1. Add the garlic, ginger, turmeric, and avocado oil to a big Dutch oven or soup pot and heat over medium heat. The aromatics should be softened after around 5 minutes of sautéing.
2. Add SunButter, red curry paste, and a little amount of vegetable broth to the saucepan. Add the sweet potatoes, chicken, and remaining vegetable broth after whisking to make a creamy paste. Allow it to boil for approximately 15 minutes, or till the chicken is cooked & the sweet potatoes become tender.
3. Regain a simmer after adding the onions, red peppers, and coconut milk. Lime juice and coconut aminos are used to season the soup. If required, taste the soup and add sea salt as desired. Give the veggies five minutes or so to soften.
4. Make zoodles using a spiralizer whilst the soup is simmering. If you do not have a spiralizer, you may just cut the zucchini or make long strands of it using a vegetable peeler.
5. To serve, top bowls with hot soup and add zoodles. If desired, add cilantro & green onions as a garnish.

PER SERVING

Total Calories: 265kcal, Fat: 10g, Carbohydrates: 24g, Protein: 20g, Fiber: 3g, Sodium: 607mg, Potassium: 665mg

Herbed Almond Turkey

Prep time: 10 minutes | Cook time:40 minutes | Serves 4

- 1 big turkey breast, skinless, boneless and cubed
- 1 tablespoon olive oil
- ½ cup chicken stock
- 1 tablespoon basil, chopped
- 1 tablespoon rosemary, chopped
- 1 tablespoon oregano, chopped
- 1 tablespoon parsley, chopped
- 3 garlic cloves, minced
- ½ cup almonds, toasted and chopped
- 3 cups tomatoes, chopped

1. Warm up a pan with the oil over medium-high heat, add the turkey and the garlic and brown for 5 minutes.
2. Add the stock and the rest of the ingredients, bring to a simmer over medium heat and cook covered for 35 minutes.
3. Divide the mix between plates and serve.

PER SERVING

Calories: 297, Fat: 11.2, Fiber: 9.2, Carbs: 19.4, Protein: 23.6 ..

Slow Cooker Delicious Chicken Mole

Prep Time: 30 minutes | Cook time: 4 hours | Serves 8

- Some salt, to taste
- 2 pounds of boneless chicken breasts
- Black pepper, to taste
- 1/2 minced yellow onion
- 2 tbsp. of avocado oil
- 4 cloves of garlic, peeled & minced
- 1/4 cup of chili powder
- 1 minced jalapeno (optional)
- 1 tsp. of cinnamon
- 2 1/2 cups of chicken broth
- 1 tsp. of cumin
- 3 tbsp. of Organic SunButter
- 1 tbsp. of arrowroot powder mix with 2 tbsp. of water
- 2 tbsp. of tomato paste
- 1 tsp. of sea salt
- 1 tbsp. of cocoa powder

1. Add the chicken to the slow cooker and season it with salt and pepper.
2. When translucent and aromatic, for approximately 6 minutes, add the minced onion, garlic, and jalapeño (if used) to a large pan with the avocado oil.
3. Stir in the salt, cumin, cinnamon, and chili powder before adding the veggies.
4. Add SunButter and tomato paste after adding the chicken broth. Blend and smooth with a whisk. Simmer for a little while.
5. Stir in the arrowroot while continuously swirling the sauce after combining it with 2 tbsp of water.
6. Chili powder & salt should be taste-tested before being added, along with the cocoa powder.
7. The sauce may now be ultra-smoothened using either an immersion or a regular blender. Even if you neglect this step, the sauce will still taste fantastic.
8. The chicken should be covered with half the sauce. Turn the crockpot to low and simmer for 4-5 hours. For serving, save the remaining sauce.
9. Take out the chicken breasts and chop or shred them.
10. To sprinkle on the chicken, reheat the remaining sauce. It may also be simply added into the slow cooker along with the chicken that has been shredded.
11. For up to three days, keep leftovers in the refrigerator. This frozen mole with shredded chicken is fantastic. For up to three months, keep in an airtight container in the freezer.

PER SERVING

Total Calories: 214kcal, Fat: 10g, Carbohydrates: 6g, Protein: 26g, Fiber: 1g, Sodium: 724mg, Potassium: 549mg ...

Chicken Scarpariello

Prep Time: 30 minutes | Cook time: 50 minutes | Serves 8

- 1 tbsp. of olive oil, plus 2 tbsp.
- 1 1/2 pounds cocktail potatoes
- Sea salt, to taste
- Black pepper, to taste
- 8 chicken thighs
- 1 yellow onion, in strips
- 3 sweet pre-cooked Italian sausages, sliced
- 1 red bell pepper, in strips
- 1 cup of white wine
- 3 cloves of garlic, minced
- 1/4 cup of white wine vinegar
- 1/2 cup of sweet pickled peppers or Peppadew peppers
- 1 cup of chicken broth
- 3 sprigs of rosemary (fresh)

1. Set the Oven to Bake Mode on 450° F for 25 minutes for 1 tray.
2. Bake some tiny potatoes on a baking sheet. Season the potatoes with Salt and pepper after drizzling them with olive oil. To uniformly coat the potatoes, use your hands.
3. While the braised chicken dish is cooking, bake the potatoes.
4. Sprinkle sea salt & pepper liberally on the chicken thighs.
5. A large Dutch oven should be heated to medium heat. Place chicken thighs in the saucepan skin side down after adding the olive oil. Give the chicken skin 5-7 minutes to brown. Chicken thighs should be taken out of the pan and placed aside.
6. Sausage should be added to the heated pan and browned for approximately five minutes. Remove and set aside the sausage.
7. Add the onions to the heated pan and lower the heat to medium-low. For approximately 5-7 minutes, as the onions start to soften, stir them. Add red bell peppers, garlic, and salt & pepper to taste. Stirring to avoid burning, soften for a further 7 to 10 minutes.
8. White wine & white wine vinegar are then added, and the mixture is simmered until it has been reduced by half.
9. Put the sausage, peppadew peppers, and chicken broth in the saucepan. The sausage is stirred into a combination of onion and pepper.
10. Place the chicken into the sausage and vegetable mixture, and then garnish with rosemary sprigs.
11. After the potatoes have been taken from the oven, set the oven to bake for 30 minutes at 350 degrees Fahrenheit.
12. Put the Dutch oven onto a tray and set the Steam Oven on the lower shelf.
13. A chicken thigh, a little pepper & onion mixture, and a teaspoon of white wine sauce should be added on top of the potatoes.

PER SERVING

Total Calories: 386kcal, Fat: 24g, Carbohydrates: 15g, Protein: 21g, Fiber: 3g, Sodium: 210mg, Potassium: 703mg

Turkey and Asparagus Mix

Prep time: 10 minutes | Cook time: 30 minutes | Serves 4

- 1 bunch asparagus, trimmed and halved
- 1 big turkey breast, skinless, boneless and cut into strips
- 1 teaspoon basil, dried
- 2 tablespoons olive oil
- A pinch of salt and black pepper
- ½ cup tomato sauce
- 1 tablespoon chives, chopped

1. Heat a pan with the oil to medium heat, then add the turkey and brown for 4 minutes.
2. Add the asparagus and the rest of the ingredients except the chives, bring to a simmer and cook over medium heat for 25 minutes.
3. Add the chives, divide the turkey mix between plates and serve.

PER SERVING

Calories: 337, Fat: 21.2, Fiber: 10.2, Carbs: 21.4, Protein: 17.6

Yogurt Chicken and Red Onion Mix

Prep time: 10 minutes | Cook time: 30 minutes | Serves 4

- 2 pounds chicken breast, skinless, boneless and sliced
- 3 tablespoons olive oil
- ¼ cup Greek yogurt
- 2 garlic cloves, minced
- ½ teaspoon onion powder
- A pinch of salt and black pepper
- 4 red onions, sliced

1. In a roasting pan, combine the chicken with the oil, the yogurt and the other ingredients, place in the oven at 375 degrees F and bake for 30 minutes.
2. Divide chicken mix between plates and serve hot.

PER SERVING

Calories: 278, Fat: 15, Fiber: 9.2, Carbs: 15.1, Protein: 23.3 ...

Lemony Turkey and Pine Nuts

Prep time: 10 minutes | Cook time: 30 minutes | Serves 4

- 2 turkey breasts, boneless, skinless and halved
- A pinch of salt and black pepper
- 2 tablespoons avocado oil
- Juice of 2 lemons
- 1 tablespoon rosemary, chopped
- 3 garlic cloves, minced
- ¼ cup pine nuts, chopped
- 1 cup chicken stock

1. Warm up a pan with the oil over medium-high heat, add the garlic and the turkey and brown for 4 minutes on each side.
2. Add the rest of the ingredients, bring to a boil and let it simmer over medium heat for 20 minutes.
3. Divide the mix between plates and serve with a side salad.

PER SERVING

Calories: 293, Fat: 12.4, Fiber: 9.3, Carbs: 17.8, Protein: 24.5

Gingery Chicken Lettuce Wraps

Prep time: 15 minutes | Cook time: 20 minutes| Serves 4

- 1-pound ground chicken
- ¼ teaspoon salt
- ¼ teaspoon freshly ground black pepper
- 3 tablespoons sesame oil, divided
- 3 tablespoons gluten-free soy sauce, tamari, or coconut aminos
- 1 bunch scallions, green and white parts separated
- 2 tablespoons minced fresh ginger
- 2 cloves garlic, minced
- ¼ teaspoon red pepper flakes
- 1 medium carrot, peeled and cut into ¼-inch dice
- 3 tablespoons rice vinegar, coconut vinegar, or apple cider vinegar
- 1 tablespoon water, plus more as needed
- Chopped fresh cilantro, for garnish Sriracha or other hot sauce (optional)
- lime wedges (optional)
-

1. Season the chicken with the salt and pepper.
2. Heat 1 tablespoon of the sesame oil in a large skillet or wok over medium-high heat. When it is hot, add the chicken and cook until browned and cooked through, stirring frequently, 3 to 4 minutes. Using a slotted spoon, transfer the cooked chicken to a bowl. Add the soy sauce and stir to combine.
3. Add 1 tablespoon of the sesame oil and the scallion whites to the pan. Cook, stirring, until the scallions are soft and translucent, about 2 minutes. Add the ginger, garlic, and red pepper flakes and cook until fragrant, 1 minute. Transfer to the bowl with the chicken and toss to combine.
4. Over medium-high heat, add the carrot and vinegar to the pan, which will steam and bubble. Add the water (and more as needed) to cover the carrot dice. Simmer until the carrot is tender and the liquid has evaporated, 3 to 4 minutes. Transfer the mixture to the bowl with the chicken and toss to combine.
5. To serve, separate the head of lettuce into leaves. Top each leaf with the chicken mixture, then add a sprinkling of the scallion greens, sesame seeds, and cilantro.
6. Serve with sriracha and lime wedges, if you like, as well as extra soy sauce.

PER SERVING

Calorie 512, Fats 24g, Carbs 18g, Protein 56g…

Turkey and Cranberry Sauce

Prep time: 10 minutes | Cook time:50 minutes | Serves 4
- 1 cup chicken stock
- 2 tablespoons avocado oil
- ½ cup cranberry sauce
- 1 big turkey breast, skinless, boneless and sliced
- 1 yellow onion, roughly chopped
- Salt and black pepper to the taste

1. Heat up a pan with the avocado oil over medium-high heat, add the onion and sauté for 5 minutes.

2. Add the turkey and brown for 5 minutes more.
3. Add the rest of the ingredients, toss, place in the pre-heated oven at 350 degrees F and cook for 40 minutes

PER SERVING

Calories: 382, Fat: 12.6, Fiber: 9.6, Carbs: 26.6, Protein: 17.6

Thyme Chicken

Prep time: 10 minutes | Cook time:50 minutes | Serves 4

- 1 tablespoon olive oil
- 4 garlic cloves, minced
- A pinch of salt and black pepper
- 2 teaspoons dried thyme
- 12 small red potatoes, halved
- 2 pounds chicken breast, skinless, boneless and cubed
- 1 cup red onion, sliced
- ¾ cup chicken stock
- 2 tablespoons basil, chopped

1. In a baking dish greased with the oil, add the potatoes, chicken and the rest of the ingredients, mix well, place in the oven and bake at 400 degrees F for 50 minutes.
2. Divide between plates and serve.

PER SERVING

Calories: 281, Fat: 9.2, Fiber: 10.9, Carbs: 21.6, Protein: 13.6

Turkey, Artichokes and Asparagus

Prep time: 10 minutes | Cook time:30 minutes | Serves 4

- 2 turkey breasts, boneless, skinless and halved
- 3 tablespoons olive oil
- 1 and ½ pounds asparagus, trimmed and halved
- 1 cup chicken stock
- A pinch of salt and black pepper
- 1 cup canned artichoke hearts, drained and roughly chopped
- ¼ cup kalamata olives, pitted and sliced
- 1 shallot, chopped
- 3 garlic cloves, minced
- 3 tablespoons dill, chopped

1. Warm up a pan with the oil over medium-high heat, add the turkey and the garlic and brown for 4 minutes on each side.
2. Add the asparagus, the stock and the rest of the ingredients except the dill, bring to a boil and simmer over medium heat for 20 minutes.
3. Add the dill, divide the mix between plates and serve.

PER SERVING

Calories: 291, Fat: 16, Fiber: 10.3, Carbs: 22.8, Protein: 34.5

Healthy Chicken Stir Fry

Prep time: 5 minutes | Cook time: 20 minutes | Serves 4

- 2 chicken breasts (large), diced
- 1 tbsp. of sesame oil
- 1 package (16 oz.) of frozen vegetables
- salt & pepper
- For stir fry sauce:
- 1 tbsp. of sesame oil
- 3 tbsp. of tamari
- 2 cloves of garlic, chopped
- ¼ tsp. of ginger
- 1 tbsp. of fish sauce
- 2 tbsp. of water or chicken broth
- 1 tsp. of sriracha
- 1 tbsp. of corn starch

1. Chicken should be diced and salted, and peppered. Place aside.
2. In a small bowl, whisk the sauce.
3. Add 1 tablespoon of sesame oil to the Instant Pot and set it to sauté. Chicken is added and cooked until it begins to brown. In the instant pot, it won't brown it that much, but some minutes should start the process.
4. Stir the sauce in the pan. Cook for 4 minutes on the manual setting of the instant pot. Turn the valve slowly to perform a rapid release when it is finished. After that, add the frozen veggies and switch the instant pot to sauté. Cook and stir until well heated.
5. Quickly serve with cauliflower rice.

PER SERVING

Total Calories: 210kcal, Fats: 9g, Carbohydrates: 3g, Protein: 25g, Fiber: 4g, Sodium: 1239mg, Potassium: 459mg ..

Sage Turkey Mix

Prep time: 10 minutes | Cook time:40 minutes | Serves 4

- 1 big turkey breast, skinless, boneless and roughly cubed
- Juice of 1 lemon
- 2 tablespoons avocado oil
- 1 red onion, chopped
- 2 tablespoons sage, chopped
- 1 garlic clove, minced
- 1 cup chicken stock

1. Heat up a pan with the avocado oil over medium-high heat, add the turkey and brown for 3 minutes on all sides.
2. Add the rest of the ingredients, let it simmer and cook over medium heat for 35 minutes.
3. Divide the turkey mix between plates and serve with a side dish.

PER SERVING

Calories: 382, Fat: 12.6, Fiber: 9.6, Carbs: 16.6, Protein: 33.2 ..

Lettuce Thai Chicken Wraps

Prep Time: 30 minutes | Cook time: 15 minutes | Serves 4

- 1 cup of red cabbage shredded
- 1 head of romaine lettuce
- 1 sliced mango
- 1/2 cup of roasted sunflower seeds, almonds, or cashews
- red chillis (optional)
- cilantro & Thai basil for garnishing
- Ginger Chicken:
- 1 pound of chicken (ground) can substitute for ground turkey
- 1 tbsp. of sesame oil
- 1/4 cup of ginger, grated (fresh)
- 2 tbsp. of coconut aminos (can substitute soy or Tamari sauce)
- 1/4 cup of minced Thai shallots
- 1/2 tbsp. of chili sauce (or some more, to taste)
- 1/4 tsp. of sea salt (or some more, to taste)
- Thai Almond Sauce
- 1/4 cup of full fat coconut milk (from can)
- 1/4 cup of sunflower seed butter or almond butter, no sugar added
- 1 tbsp. of rice wine vinegar
- 1/2 tbsp. of lime juice, fresh (1/2 large lime)
- 1 1/2 tbsp. of coconut aminos
- 1/2 tsp. of chilli sauce
- A pinch salt, to taste
- 1 tsp. of sesame oil

1. Sesame oil is heated in a pan over medium-high heat, then ginger and shallots are added to prepare the chicken. Cook until extremely soft and aromatic, 7 to 10 minutes.
2. Brown the ground chicken after adding it. To taste, add coconut aminos, sea salt, and chilli sauce.
3. Blend all the ingredients together to create the SunButter sauce. While a blender may make it more quickly, you can also make it using a bowl & a little whisk. The SunButter sauce should be refrigerated until used.
4. Add the chicken, mango, and cabbage to the wraps before adding the toasted nuts and herbs.
5. Serve with a side of hot SunButter sauce or drizzle some over.

PER SERVING

Total Calories: 497kcal, Fat: 33g, Carbohydrates: 26g, Protein: 28g, Fiber: 6g, Sodium: 559mg, Potassium: 1381mg

Chicken Fennel Bake

Prep time: 15 minutes | Cook time: 55 minutes| Serves 2

- 5 lemons
- ¼ cup extra-virgin olive oil
- 1 lb.(s) baby potatoes
- 2 fennel bulbs, trimmed
- Kosher salt and freshly ground black pepper
- 1 cup baby carrots
- 6 chicken thighs

1. Preheat the oven to 375°F. Line a baking sheet with foil.
2. Cut the fennel into thick slices. Shingle them onto the center of the baking sheet and season with salt and pepper.
3. Set aside 2 Zest lemons and set aside, then juice these lemons into a medium bowl.
4. Whisk the olive oil into the lemon juice and season with salt and pepper.
5. Halve the remaining 3 lemons and add them to the bowl along with the potatoes and carrots. Toss to coat.
6. Spread the vegetables and lemon halves around the outside of the baking sheet. Put the chicken thighs in the same bowl along with the reserved lemon zest and more salt and pepper. Toss to coat.
7. Put the chicken on top of the fennel skin-side up, leaving a little space between pieces.
8. Bake, stirring the potatoes and carrots halfway through, until the chicken is cooked through and the vegetables are tender, 50 minutes to 1 hour.
9. Serve the chicken with the vegetables and roasted lemon halves.

PER SERVING

Calorie 520, Fats 55g, Carbs 13g, Protein 21g..

Chapter 8
Pork, Beef and Lamb

Picadillo Stuffed Bell Peppers

Prep time: 5 minutes | Cook time: 25 minutes| Serves 4

- 2 red, yellow, orange, or green bell peppers
- 3 tablespoons extra-virgin olive oil, divided
- 1-pound ground chicken or ground grass-fed beef
- 1 tablespoon ground cumin
- 1 tablespoon chili powder
- 1½ teaspoons ground cinnamon
- ¼ teaspoon salt
- ¼ teaspoon freshly ground black pepper
- Pinch cayenne pepper (optional)
- 1 small yellow or sweet onion, diced
- 2 cloves garlic, minced
- 6 plum tomatoes, diced, juices reserved
- 1 cup pitted or pimento-stuffed green olives, quartered
- ½ cup chopped fresh cilantro

1. Preheat the oven to 400°F.
2. Slice the peppers in half, keeping the stem intact, and remove seeds. Lightly coat with 1 tablespoon olive oil and place on an aluminum foil–lined baking sheet, cut-side up.
3. In a medium bowl, mix the meat with the cumin, chili powder, cinnamon, salt, black pepper, and cayenne (if using).
4. Heat 1 tablespoon of the oil in a large skillet over medium heat. Add the meat and cook until lightly browned but not cooked through, about 2 minutes. Transfer to a bowl using a slotted spoon.
5. In the same skillet, heat the remaining 1 tablespoon oil. Add the onion and cook until soft and translucent, stirring a few times, about 2 minutes. Add the garlic and cook until fragrant, about 30 seconds.
6. Stir in the tomatoes and their juices, olives, and cilantro. Spoon the mixture into the bell pepper halves.
7. Bake until the peppers are tender and any excess tomato juices have evaporated, 10 to 15 minutes. Remove from the oven, allow to cool slightly, and serve.

PER SERVING

Calorie 768, Fats 49g, Carbs 29g, Protein 51g...

Brined Pork Chops with Caramelized Apple Onion Relish

Prep time: 15 minutes | Cook time: 20 minutes| Serves 4

- Brined Pork
- 1½ cups water
- ½ cup apple cider vinegar
- 2 tablespoons salt, plus more for seasoning
- 1 teaspoon freshly ground black pepper (or ½ tablespoon peppercorns), plus more for seasoning
- 1 teaspoon maple syrup
- 2 (2-inch-thick) bone-in pastured pork chops
- Relish
- 1 medium red apple
- 1 teaspoon lemon juice
- 2 tablespoons unsalted grass-fed butter
- 1 tablespoon olive oil
- 1 medium yellow onion, diced
- 2 cloves garlic, minced
- 2 tablespoons chopped fresh parsley (optional)

1. In a large shallow bowl, combine the water, vinegar, salt, pepper, and maple syrup and microwave on high until the salt dissolves, about 1 minute.
2. Add the pork, submerging it in the brine. Cover and refrigerate for at least an hour and up to overnight.
3. Place a baking sheet or broiler pan in the oven and set the broiler to high. Remove the chops from the brine, shaking off any excess and patting dry. Season each side evenly with salt and pepper and set aside to dry out further while you prepare the relish.
4. For the relish, dice the apple and toss with the lemon juice. Heat the butter and oil in a medium skillet over medium heat.
5. Add the onion and cook, stirring occasionally, until it starts to caramelize, 7 to 10 minutes. Add the garlic and cook until fragrant, about 30 seconds.
6. Reduce the heat to low, add the apple, stir to coat with the mixture, cover the pan, and cook until just warmed, 1 to 2 minutes.
7. Remove from the heat, stir in the parsley (if using), and set aside.
8. Transfer the pork chops to a baking sheet or broiler pan and broil until slightly pink in the center, about 3 minutes per side, reserving juices from the pan. Let rest for 3 minutes.
9. To serve, divide the chops between two plates. Pour any juice from the pan over the chops, top evenly with the apple-onion relish, and serve.

PER SERVING

Calorie 444, Fats 28g, Carbs 25g, Protein 25g..

Shawarma Pork Tenderloin with Pitas

Prep time: 15 minutes | Cook time: 35 minutes | Serves 8

- For the shawarma spice rub:
- 1 teaspoon ground cumin
- 1 teaspoon ground coriander
- 1 teaspoon ground turmeric
- ¾ teaspoon sweet Spanish paprika
- ½ teaspoon ground cloves
- ¼ teaspoon salt
- ¼ teaspoon freshly ground black pepper
- 1/8 teaspoon ground cinnamon
- For the shawarma:
- 1½ pounds pork tenderloin
- 3 tablespoons extra-virgin olive oil
- 1 tablespoon garlic powder
- Salt
- Freshly ground black pepper
- 1½ tablespoons Shawarma Spice Rub
- 4 pita pockets, halved, for serving
- 1 to 2 tomatoes, sliced, for serving
- ¼ cup pickled onions, for serving
- ¼ cup pickled turnips, for serving
- ¼ cup store-bought hummus or garlic-lemon hummus

1. To Make the Shawarma Seasoning:
2. In a small bowl, combine the cumin, coriander, turmeric, paprika, cloves, salt, pepper, and cinnamon and set aside.
3. To Make the Shawarma:
4. Preheat the oven to 400°F. Put the pork tenderloin on a plate and cover with olive oil and garlic powder on each side.
5. Season with salt and pepper and rub each side of the tenderloin with a generous amount of shawarma spices.
6. Place the pork tenderloin in the center of a roasting pan and roast for 20 minutes per pound, or until the meat begins to bounce back as you poke it.
7. If it feels like there's still fluid under the skin, continue cooking. Check every 5 to 7 minutes until it reaches the desired tenderness and juices run clear.
8. Remove the pork from the oven and let rest for 10 minutes. Serve the pork tenderloin shawarma with pita pockets, tomatoes, Pickled Onions (if using), Pickled Turnips (if using), and hummus.

PER SERVING

Calories: 316 Protein: 29g Carbs: 17g Fat: 15g.

Lamb Burger

Prep time: 15 minutes | Cook time: 15 minutes | Serves 4

- 1-pound ground lamb
- ½ small red onion, grated
- 1 tablespoon dried parsley
- 1 teaspoon dried oregano
- 1 teaspoon ground cumin
- 1 teaspoon garlic powder
- ½ teaspoon dried mint
- ¼ teaspoon paprika
- ¼ teaspoon kosher salt
- 1/8 teaspoon freshly ground black pepper
- Extra-virgin olive oil, for panfrying
- 4 pita breads, for serving (optional)
- Tzatziki Sauce, for serving (optional)
- pickled onions, for serving (optional)

1. In a bowl, combine the lamb, onion, parsley, oregano, cumin, garlic powder, mint, paprika, salt, and pepper. Divide the meat into 4 small balls and work into smooth discs.
2. In a large sauté pan or skillet, heat a drizzle of olive oil over medium heat or brush a grill with oil and set it too medium.
3. Cook the patties for 4 to 5 minutes on each side, until cooked through and juices run clear. Enjoy lamb burgers in pitas, topped with tzatziki sauce and pickled onions (if using).

PER SERVING

Calories: 328 Protein: 19g Carbs: 2g Fat: 27g.

Mediterranean Lamb Bowl

Prep time: 15 minutes | Cook time: 15 minutes | Serves 2

- 2 tablespoons extra-virgin olive oil
- ¼ cup diced yellow onion
- 1-pound ground lamb
- 1 teaspoon dried mint
- 1 teaspoon dried parsley
- ½ teaspoon red pepper flakes
- ¼ teaspoon garlic powder
- 1 cup cooked rice
- ½ teaspoon za'atar seasoning
- ½ cup halved cherry tomatoes
- 1 cucumber, peeled and diced
- 1 cup store-bought hummus or Garlic-Lemon Hummus
- 1 cup crumbled feta cheese
- 2 pita breads, warmed (optional)

1. In a large sauté pan or skillet, heat the olive oil over medium heat and cook the onion for about 2 minutes, until fragrant.
2. Add the lamb and mix well, breaking up the meat as you cook. Once the lamb is halfway cooked, add mint, parsley, red pepper flakes, and garlic powder.
3. In a medium bowl, mix together the cooked rice and za'atar, then divide between individual serving bowls. Add the seasoned lamb, then top the bowls with the tomatoes, cucumber, hummus, feta, and pita (if using).

PER SERVING

Calories: 1,312 Protein: 62g Carbs: 62g Fat: 96g.

Marinated Lamb Kebabs with Crunchy Yogurt Dressing

Prep time: 15 minutes| Cook time: 15 minutes| Serves 4

½ cup plain, unsweetened, full-fat Greek yogurt
- ¼ cup extra-virgin olive oil
- ¼ cup freshly squeezed lemon juice
- 1 teaspoon grated lemon zest
- 2 garlic cloves, minced
- 2 tablespoons honey
- 2 tablespoons balsamic vinegar
- 1½ teaspoons oregano, fresh, minced
- 1 teaspoon thyme, fresh, minced
- 1 bay leaf
- 1 teaspoon kosher salt
- ½ teaspoon freshly ground black pepper
- ½ teaspoon red pepper flakes
- 2 pounds' leg of lamb, trimmed, cleaned and cut into 1-inch pieces
- 1 large red onion, diced large
- 1 recipe crunchy yogurt dip
- parsley, chopped, for garnish
- lemon wedges, for garnish

1. In a bowl or large resealable bag, combine the yogurt, olive oil, lemon juice and zest, garlic, honey, balsamic vinegar, oregano, thyme, bay leaf, salt, pepper, and red pepper flakes. Mix well.
2. Add the lamb pieces and marinate, refrigerated, for 30 minutes. Preheat the oven to 375°F. Thread the lamb onto the skewers, alternating with chunks of red onion as desired.
3. Put the skewers onto a baking sheet and roast for 10 to 15 minutes, rotating every 5 minutes to ensure that they cook evenly.
4. Plate the skewers and allow them to rest briefly. Top or serve with the yogurt dressing. To finish, garnish with fresh chopped parsley and a lemon wedge.

PER SERVING

Calories: 578 Protein: 56g Carbs: 20g Fat: 30g.

Moroccan Pot Roast

Prep time: 15 minutes| Cook time: 50 minutes| Serves 4

- 8 ounces mushrooms, sliced
- 4 tablespoons extra-virgin olive oil
- 3 small onions, cut into 2-inch pieces
- 2 tablespoons paprika
- 1½ tablespoons garam masala
- 2 teaspoons salt
- ¼ teaspoon ground white pepper
- 2 tablespoons tomato paste
- 1 small eggplant, peeled and diced
- 1¼ cups low-sodium beef broth
- ½ cup halved apricots
- 1/3 cup golden raisins
- 3 pounds' beef chuck roast
- 2 tablespoons honey
- 1 tablespoon dried mint
- 2 cups cooked brown rice

1. Set an electric pressure cooker to Sauté and put the mushrooms and oil in the cooker. Sauté for 5 min-

utes, then add the onions, paprika, garam masala, salt, and white pepper. Stir in the tomato paste and continue to sauté.
2. Add the eggplant and sauté for 5 more minutes, until softened. Pour in the broth. Add the apricots and raisins. Sear the meat for 2 minutes on each side. Close and lock the lid and set the pressure cooker too high for 50 minutes.
3. When cooking is complete, quick release the pressure. Carefully remove the lid, then remove the meat from the sauce and break it into pieces. While the meat is removed, stir honey and mint into the sauce.
4. Assemble plates with ½ cup of brown rice, ½ cup of pot roast sauce, and 3 to 5 pieces of pot roast.

PER SERVING

Calories: 829 Protein: 69g Carbs: 70g Fat: 34g.

Curried Beef with Winter Vegetables

Prep time: 15 minutes | Cook time: 40 minutes| Serves 4

- 2 potatoes, peeled and cubed
- 1 zucchini, sliced
- 2 apples - peeled, cored and chopped
- 3 cloves garlic, minced
- 2 onions, peeled and diced
- 1 teaspoon ground turmeric
- 2 carrots, peeled and sliced
- parsnips, peeled and sliced
- 2 celery ribs, chopped
- 2 tablespoons curry powder, or to taste
- 2 teaspoons coriander powder
- 1 teaspoon Asian five-spice powder
- 1/2-pound beef for stew, such as beef chuck roast, cut into 1-inch chunks
- 3 tablespoons olive oil
- 2 (3 inch) pieces fresh ginger root, peeled and diced
- 1 cup raisins1 cup cashews
- 1/2 cup water

1. Preheat oven to 350 degrees F (175 degrees C). Line a roasting pan with aluminum foil.
2. Place the beef into a pan with enough water to cover. Bring to a boil, reduce heat and simmer for 30 minutes.
3. Meanwhile, heat the olive oil in a deep pot over medium-high heat. Stir in the ginger, garlic, onions, and celery, and cook until vegetables soften, about 5 minutes.
4. Mix in the curry powder, coriander powder, five-spice powder, and turmeric, and toss to evenly coat the onion mixture.
5. Cook about 5 minutes more, and stir in the carrots, parsnips, potatoes, zucchini, and apples. Stir in the beef with its cooking liquid, raisins, and cashews, and toss to evenly blend the spices.
6. Pour the beef and vegetable mixture into the prepared roasting pan. Drizzle 1/2 cup water over the mixture. Cover the pan with aluminum foil.
7. Bake in preheated oven until heated through, about 1 hour.

PER SERVING

Calorie 343, Fats 17.5g, Carbs 40.7g, Protein 10.3g.

Moussaka

Prep time: 15 minutes| Cook time: 40 minutes| Serves 6-8

For the eggplant:
- 2 pounds' eggplant, cut into ¼-inch-thick slices
- 1 teaspoon salt
- 2 to 3 tablespoons extra-virgin olive oil
- For the filling:
- 1 tablespoon extra-virgin olive oil
- 2 shallots, diced
- 1 tablespoon dried, minced garlic
- 1-pound ground lamb
- 4 ounces portobello mushrooms, diced
- 1 (14.5-ounce) can crushed tomatoes, drained
- ¼ cup tomato paste
- 1 cup low-sodium beef broth
- 2 bay leaves
- 2 teaspoons dried oregano
- ¾ teaspoon salt
- 2½ cups store-bought béchamel sauce
- 1/3 cup panko bread crumbs

To Make the Eggplant
1. Preheat the oven to 450°F. Line large baking sheets with paper towels and arrange the eggplant slices in a single layer and sprinkle with salt.
2. Place another layer of paper towel on the eggplant slices. Continue until all eggplant slices are covered.
3. Let the eggplant sweat for 30 minutes to remove excess moisture. While this is happening, make the meat sauce.
4. Pat the eggplant dry. Dry the baking sheets and brush with oil and place the eggplant slices onto the baking sheets.
5. Bake for 15 to 20 minutes, or until lightly browned and softened. Remove from the oven and cool slightly before assembling the moussaka.
6. To Make the Filling
7. In a large, oven-safe sauté pan or skillet, heat the olive oil over high heat. Cook the shallots and garlic for 2 minutes, until starting to soften.
8. Add the ground lamb and brown it with the garlic and onions, breaking it up as it cooks. Add the mushrooms and cook for 5 to 7 minutes, or until they have dehydrated slightly.
9. Add the tomatoes and paste, beef broth, bay leaves, oregano, and salt and stir to combine.
10. Once the sauce is simmering, lower to medium-low and cook for 15 minutes, or until it reduces to a thick sauce. Remove the sauce to a separate bowl before assembly.
11. Reduce the oven temperature to 350°F. Place half the eggplant slices in the bottom of the skillet used to make the sauce. Top the slices with all the meat filling.
12. Place the remaining eggplant on top of the meat filling and pour the jarred béchamel sauce over the eggplant. Sprinkle with the bread crumbs.
13. Bake for 30 to 40 minutes or until golden brown. Let stand for 10 minutes before serving.

PER SERVING

Calories: 491 Protein: 23g Carbs: 30g Fat: 33g.

Flank Steak with Artichokes

Prep time: 15 minutes| Cook time: 60 minutes| Serves 4-6

- 4 tablespoons grapeseed oil, divided
- 2 pounds' flank steak
- 1 (14-ounce) can artichoke hearts, drained and roughly chopped
- 1 onion, diced
- 8 garlic cloves, chopped
- 1 (32-ounce) container low-sodium beef broth
- 1 (14.5-ounce) can diced tomatoes, drained
- 1 cup tomato sauce
- 2 tablespoons tomato paste
- 1 teaspoon dried oregano
- 1 teaspoon dried parsley
- 1 teaspoon dried basil
- ½ teaspoon ground cumin
- 3 bay leaves
- 2 to 3 cups cooked couscous (optional)

1. Preheat the oven to 450°f. In an oven-safe sauté pan or skillet, heat 3 tablespoons of oil on medium heat.
2. Sear the steak for 2 minutes per side on both sides. Transfer the steak to the oven for 30 minutes, or until desired tenderness.
3. Meanwhile, in a large pot, combine the remaining 1 tablespoon of oil, artichoke hearts, onion, and garlic.
4. Pour in the beef broth, tomatoes, tomato sauce, and tomato paste. Stir in oregano, parsley, basil, cumin, and bay leaves.
5. Cook the vegetables, covered, for 30 minutes. Remove bay leaf and serve with flank steak and ½ cup of couscous per plate, if using.

PER SERVING

Calories: 577 Protein: 55g Carbs: 22g Fat: 28g.

Korean Beef Bowl

Prep time: 15 minutes| Cook time: 15 minutes| Serves 4

- 2" of peeled fresh ginger, grated
- 1 teaspoon of onion powder
- 1 tablespoon of sesame oil, toasted
- 2 pounds of ground beef
- 1 diced shallot
- 1 teaspoon of red pepper flakes
- 1 teaspoon of garlic powder
- Half cup of coconut aminos
- 2 cups of mixed greens
- 2 tablespoons of fish sauce
- 4 cups of cauliflower rice

1. In a skillet, heat oil on medium flame.
2. Add beef and break it into small pieces.
3. Add ginger, onion, garlic powder, red pepper and shallots. Cook for 8 minutes.
4. Add fish sauce, coconut aminos and cook for 3 to 4 minutes.
5. Serve beef with cauliflower rice and mixed greens.

PER SERVING

Calories: 392 Total fat: 12 g Total carbs: 7 g Fiber: 6.9 g Sugar: 4.1 g Protein: 38 g Sodium: 397 mg.

Beef Curry Stew

Prep time: 15 minutes | Cook time: 8 hours 10 minutes | Serves 4

- 1 pound of beef stew meat
- 1 tbsp. of olive oil
- salt & pepper to taste
- 1 tsp. of chopped fresh ginger
- 2 cloves of garlic, minced
- 1 jalapeno pepper (fresh), diced
- 1 can of diced tomatoes (14.5 ounces) with juice
- 1 tbsp. of curry powder
- 1 cup of beef broth
- 1 sliced onion, quartered

1. The steak should be browned evenly in a pan over medium heat with olive oil. Season with salt & pepper after removing from the pan and conserving the juices. Curry powder is added after cooking and stirring the ginger, garlic, and jalapeño in the pan for 2 minutes, or until they are soft. Add the juice and chopped tomatoes together.
2. The browned meat should be layered on top of the onion into the bottom of the slow cooker. Add the beef broth after transferring the skillet mixture to the slow cooker.
3. Cook for 6-8 hours on Low with a cover.

PER SERVING

Total Calories: 291kcal, Fats: 19.1g, Carbohydrates: 7.6g, Protein: 20.6g, Fiber: 2g, Sodium: 441.7mg, Potassium: 460.7mg.

Basil Parmesan Pork Roast

Prep time: 10 minutes | Cook time:2 Hours | Serves 8

- 2 lbs. lean pork roast, boneless
- 1 tablespoon parsley
- ½ cup parmesan cheese, grated
- 28 oz. can tomato, diced
- 1 teaspoon dried oregano
- 1 teaspoon dried basil
- 1 teaspoon garlic powder
- Pepper
- Salt
1. Add the meat into the crock pot.
2. Mix together tomatoes, oregano, basil, garlic powder, parsley, cheese, pepper, and salt and pour over meat.
3. Cook on low for 6 hours.
4. Serve and enjoy.

PER SERVING

Calories 294 Fat 11.6 g Carbohydrates 5 g Protein 38 g .

Garlic Pork Tenderloin and Lemony Orzo

Prep time: 15 minutes| Cook time: 20 minutes| Serves 6

- 1-pound pork tenderloin
- ½ teaspoon Shawarma Spice Rub
- 1 tablespoon salt

- ½ teaspoon coarsely ground black pepper
- ½ teaspoon garlic powder
- 6 tablespoons extra-virgin olive oil
- 3 cups Lemony Orzo

1. Preheat the oven to 350°F. Rub the pork with shawarma seasoning, salt, pepper, and garlic powder and drizzle with the olive oil.
2. Put the pork on a baking sheet and roast for 20 minutes, or until desired doneness. Remove the pork from the oven and let rest for 10 minutes. Assemble the pork on a plate with the orzo and enjoy.

PER SERVING

Calories: 579 Protein: 33g Carbs: 37g Fat: 34g.

Short Beef Ribs

Prep time: 5 minutes | Cook time: 45 minutes | Serves 6

- 1 chopped onion
- 6 short ribs of beef (about 3 to 3 ½ pounds)
- 3 garlic cloves, diced
- ½ tsp. of dried thyme
- 2 tbsp. of tomato paste
- ½ tsp. of dried rosemary
- 1 ½ cups of beef broth
- 1 tbsp. of avocado oil or olive oil
- 1 ½ tbsp. of corn starch (or almond flour)
- ½ tsp. of pepper
- ¾ tsp. of Kosher salt

1. Salt and pepper the short ribs liberally.
2. Add 1 tablespoon of olive oil to the sauté setting on the Instant Pot. Brown Ribs. Allow them to remain still on each side so they would have time to brown. Around 8-10 minutes.
3. Remove the ribs. If the pan is dry, add some more oil. Sauté the onions, garlic, and other delicious ingredients at the bottom of the pan. Add all ingredients but cornstarch after sautéing for around 5 minutes. Reposition the ribs in the sauce.
4. Set the Instant Pot to stew setting and secure the cover. Organize a 30-minute timer. Allow the pot to naturally release once the timer whistles; do not open. The ribs get sensitive at this point. You must add 15-20 minutes to the preparation time if you use bone-in ribs.
5. Turn the pot to sauté after removing the meat into a platter. In a small dish, combine the cornstarch with 2-3 tablespoons of water and stir thoroughly. Add to the sauce in the pan's bottom and stir thoroughly. Remove all of the brown residues from the pan's bottom. Cook food until the desired thickness.
6. Serve with rice, mashed potatoes, or cauliflower mash. To taste, add salt and pepper.

PER SERVING

Total Calories: 49kcal, Fats: 2g, Carbohydrates: 5g, Protein: 1g, Fiber: 2g, Sodium: 558mg, Potassium: 119mg.

Red Pepper Pork Tenderloin

Prep time: 10 minutes | Cook time:25 minutes | Serves 4

- 1 lb. pork tenderloin
- 3/4 teaspoon red pepper
- 2 teaspoon dried oregano
- 1 tablespoon olive oil
- 3 tablespoon feta cheese, crumbled
- 3 tablespoon olive tapenades

1. Add pork, oil, red pepper, and oregano in a zip-lock bag and rub well and place in a refrigerator for 2 hours.
2. Remove pork from zip-lock bag. Using sharp knife make lengthwise cut through the center of the tenderloin.
3. Spread olive tapenade on half tenderloin and sprinkle with feta cheese.
4. Fold another half of meat over to the original shape of the tenderloin.
5. Tie the pork tenderloin with twine at 2-inch intervals.
6. Grill the pork tenderloin for 20 minutes.
7. Cut into slices and serve with some vegetables.

PER SERVING

Calories 215 Fat 9.1 g Carbohydrates 1 g Protein 30.8 g ..

Roasted Pork with Apple-Dijon Sauce

Prep time: 15 minutes| Cook time: 40 minutes| Serves 8

- 1½ tablespoons extra-virgin olive oil
- 1 (12-ounce) pork tenderloin
- ¼ teaspoon kosher salt
- ¼ teaspoon freshly ground black pepper
- ¼ cup apple jelly
- ¼ cup apple juice
- 2 to 3 tablespoons Dijon mustard
- ½ tablespoon corn starch
- ½ tablespoon cream

1. Preheat the oven to 325°F. In a large sauté pan or skillet, heat the olive oil over medium heat.
2. Add the pork to the skillet, using tongs to turn and sear the pork on all sides. Once seared, sprinkle pork with salt and pepper, and set it on a small baking sheet.
3. In the same skillet, with the juices from the pork, mix the apple jelly, juice, and mustard into the pan juices. Heat thoroughly over low heat, stirring consistently for 5 minutes. Spoon over the pork.
4. Put the pork in the oven and roast for 15 to 17 minutes, or 20 minutes per pound. Every 10 to 15 minutes, baste the pork with the apple-mustard sauce.
5. Once the pork tenderloin is done, remove it from the oven and let it rest for 15 minutes. Then, cut it into 1-inch slices.
6. In a small pot, blend the cornstarch with cream. Heat over low heat. Add the pan juices into the pot, stirring for 2 minutes, until thickened. Serve the sauce over the pork.

PER SERVING

Calories: 146 Protein: 13g Carbs: 8g Fat: 7g..

Baked Thai Pork Tenderloin

Prep Time: 15 minutes | Cook time: 15 minutes | Serves 6

- 3 tbsp. of rice wine vinegar
- 2 tbsp. of soy sauce or 1/4 cup of coconut aminos + 2 tbsp. of water
- 3 tbsp. of lime juice
- 2 tbsp. of coconut sugar
- 2 tbsp. of sesame oil
- 2 tbsp. of grated ginger; fresh
- 1 tbsp. of paleo Sriracha
- 1 tbsp. of garlic, minced
- 2 pounds of pork tenderloin
- 1 tsp. of sea salt

1. In a bowl, mix all the ingredients with the exception of the pork.
2. Put the pork tenderloin with the marinade in an airtight container. Turning tenderloin over periodically will help ensure even marinating. Marinate for two hours overnight.
3. The oven should be preheated to 485°.
4. Turn the oven's broil setting on if using a standard oven.
5. Put the remaining marinade into a small saucepan, then pour it over the pork in the baking dish.
6. For a medium-cooked pork tenderloin, bake the meat for 15 minutes, or till the internal temperature reads 145°F. .
7. Turn over the tenderloin halfway through baking and check the internal temperature then and every three to four minutes after that, if using a regular oven set to broil.
8. The marinade should be heated to a simmer over low heat, stirring regularly, and simmering until it has reduced by half.
9. To get rid of the ginger and garlic pieces, pour the marinade using a mesh strainer.
10. Prior to slicing, let the meat 10 minutes to rest. Serve along with the sauce or drizzle it with the reduced sauce.

PER SERVING

Total Calories: 253kcal, Fat: 10g, Carbohydrates: 7g, Protein: 31g, Fiber: 1g, Sodium: 701mg, Potassium: 613mg ..

Greek Beef Roast

Prep time: 10 minutes | Cook time:2 Hours | Serves 6

- 2 lbs. lean top round beef roast
- 1 tablespoon Italian seasoning
- 6 garlic cloves, minced
- 1 onion, sliced
- 2 cups beef broth
- ½ cup red wine
- 1 teaspoon red pepper flakes
- Pepper
- Salt

1. Season meat with pepper and salt and place into a pot.
2. Pour remaining ingredients over meat.
3. Cover, bring to a boil and then cook on low flame for 2 hours.
4. Slice the meat, dress with cooking sauce and serve.

PER SERVING

Calories 231 Fat 6 g Carbohydrates 4 g Protein 35 g ..

Jalapeno Lamb Patties

Prep time: 10 minutes | Cook time:8 minutes | Serves 4

- 1 lb. ground lamb
- 1 jalapeno pepper, minced
- 5 basil leaves, minced
- 10 mint leaves, minced
- ¼ cup fresh parsley, chopped
- 1 cup feta cheese, crumbled
- 1 tablespoon garlic, minced
- 1 teaspoon dried oregano
- ¼ teaspoon pepper
- ½ teaspoon kosher salt

1. Add all ingredients into a mixing bowl and mix until well combined.
2. Preheat the grill to 450 F.
3. Spray grill grates with cooking spray.
4. Make four equal shape patties from meat mixture, place on hot grill and cook for 3 minutes. Carefully flip the patties over and cook for a further 4 minutes.
5. Serve and enjoy.

PER SERVING

Calories 317 Fat 16 g Carbohydrates 3 g Protein 37.5 g ..

Beef and Chili Mix

Prep time: 15 minutes| Cook time: 16 Minutes | Serves 4

- 2 green chili peppers
- 8 oz beef flank steak
- 1 teaspoon salt
- 2 tablespoons olive oil
- 1 teaspoon apple cider vinegar

Pour olive oil in the skillet. Place the flank steak in the oil and roast it for 3 minutes from each side. Then sprinkle the meat with salt and apple cider vinegar.

1. Chop the chili peppers and add them in the skillet. Fry the beef for 10 minutes more. Stir it from time to time.

PER SERVING

Calories: 166 Fat 10.5g Carbs 0.2g Protein17.2g

Easy Honey-Garlic Pork Chops

Prep time: 15 minutes| Cook time: 25 minutes| Serves 4

- 4 pork chops, boneless or bone-in
- ¼ teaspoon salt
- 1/8 teaspoon freshly ground black pepper
- 3 tablespoons extra-virgin olive oil
- 5 tablespoons low-sodium chicken broth, divided
- 6 garlic cloves, minced
- ¼ cup honey
- 2 tablespoons apple cider vinegar

1. Season the pork chops with salt and pepper and set aside.
2. In a large sauté pan or skillet, heat the oil over medium-high heat. Add the pork chops and sear for 5 minutes on each side, or until golden brown.
3. Once the searing is complete, move the pork to a dish and reduce the skillet heat from medium-high to medium.
4. Add 3 tablespoons of chicken broth to the pan; this will loosen the bits and flavors from the bottom of the skillet.
5. Once the broth has evaporated, add the garlic to the skillet and cook for 15 to 20 seconds, until fragrant.
6. Add the honey, vinegar, and the remaining 2 tablespoons of broth. Bring the heat back up to medium-high and continue to cook for 3 to 4 minutes.
7. Stir periodically; the sauce is ready once it's thickened slightly. Add the pork chops back into the pan, cover them with the sauce, and cook for 2 minutes. Serve.

PER SERVING

Calories: 302 Protein: 22g Carbs: 19g Fat: 16g

Tomato Pork Chops

Prep time: 10 minutes | Cook time:1 hour 10 minutes | Serves 4

- 4 pork chops, bone-in
- 1 tablespoon garlic, minced
- ½ small onion, chopped
- 6 oz. can tomato paste
- 1 bell pepper, chopped
- ¼ teaspoon red pepper flakes
- 1 teaspoon Worcestershire sauce
- 1 tablespoon dried Italian seasoning
- 14.5 oz. can tomato, diced
- 2 teaspoon olive oil
- ¼ teaspoon pepper
- 1 teaspoon kosher salt

1. Warmth oil in a pan over medium-high heat.
2. Season pork chops with pepper and salt.
3. Sear pork chops in pan until brown on both sides.
4. Transfer the pork chops into a pot.
5. Add the remaining ingredients to the pot.
6. Cover and cook on low flame for 1 hour.
7. Remove the lid and roast for about 10 minutes.
8. Serve and enjoy.

PER SERVING

Calories 325 Fat 23.4 g Carbohydrates 10 g Protein 20 g

Vietnamese Beef with Lettuce Wraps

Prep Time: 30 minutes | Cook time: 10 minutes | Serves 4

- 1 tsp. of sea salt
- 12 ounces of sirloin steaks (grass-fed)
- 3 tbsp. of coconut aminos
- 3 tbsp. of minced lemongrass finely
- 3 tbsp. of lime juice
- 2 cloves of garlic, finely minced
- 1 finely minced shallot
- Peanut Vietnamese Sauce:
- 1/4 cup of coconut milk
- 1/4 cup of Butter (No Sugar Added)
- 1/4 cup of coconut aminos
- 2 tbsp. of lime juice
- 2 tbsp. of rice wine vinegar
- 1-3 tbsp. of paleo sriracha
- 1 tbsp. of sesame oil
- Lettuce Beef Wraps:
- 1 cup of carrots julienned
- 1 head of butter lettuce
- 1 cup of thinly sliced purple cabbage
- 1/2 cup of fresh mint
- 1 cup of fresh basil
- 2 tbsp. of sesame seeds to garnish (optional)

1. To coat the steaks, combine the marinade ingredients with the steaks in an airtight container. For up to 24 hours, marinate. The steak may be thinly sliced and marinated for an hour if you do not have the time to prepare them a day in advance.

2. Peanut Sauce
3. Blend the sauce ingredients in a blender until completely smooth. Until you are ready to use, set away, or chill. The remaining sauce is excellent as a salad dressing or vegetable dip and keeps well in the fridge for about a week.
4. Beef Lettuce Wraps:
5. On a dish, arrange lettuce leaves and then garnish with herbs and veggies.
6. If at all feasible, cook the steak outside to the desired doneness. If grilling outside isn't an option, sear the steak on both sides in a cast iron skillet that has been oiled with avocado oil over high heat. Cook at a lower temperature as desired until desired doneness.
7. Before slicing, let the steak rest for 8-10 minutes with the foil covering it. Divide the thinly sliced meat among the lettuce leaves. If desired, top with sesame seeds.

PER SERVING

Total Calories: 364kcal, Fat: 21g, Carbohydrates: 22g, Protein: 25g. Fiber: 3g, Sodium: 1260mg, Potassium: 717mg

Pork with Tomato & Olives

Prep time: 10 minutes | Cook time:30 minutes | Serves 6

- 6 pork chops, boneless
- 1/8 teaspoon ground cinnamon
- 1/2 cup olives, pitted and sliced
- 8 oz. can tomato, crushed
- 1/4 cup beef broth
- 2 garlic cloves, chopped
- 1 large onion, sliced
- 1 tablespoon olive oil

1. Warm up olive oil in a pan over medium heat.
2. Place pork chops in a pan and cook until lightly brown on both sides and set aside.
3. Cook garlic and onion in the same pan over medium heat until onion is softened.
4. Add broth and bring to boil over high heat.
5. Return pork to pan and stir in crushed tomatoes and remaining ingredients.
6. Cover and simmer for 20 minutes.
7. Serve and enjoy.

PER SERVING

Calories 321 Fat 23 g Carbohydrates 7 g Protein 19 g ..

Sheet Pan Pork Tenderloin with Brussels Sprouts, Sweet Onion, and Rosemary

Prep time: 5 minutes | Cook time: 20 minutes| Serves 4
Pork
- 1 (1-pound) pork tenderloin
- 1 teaspoon salt
- 1 teaspoon freshly ground black pepper
- 1 teaspoon paprika (regular or smoked, optional)
- Brussels Sprouts
- 1-pound Brussels sprouts, trimmed and halved
- 1 medium yellow or sweet onion, cut into ½-inch wedges
- 2 tablespoons extra-virgin olive oil
- 1 teaspoon maple syrup
- 1 tablespoon fresh rosemary, minced

1. Preheat the oven to 425°F. Line a baking sheet with aluminum foil or parchment paper.
2. Place the pork in the center of the prepared baking sheet and pat dry. Mix the salt, pepper, and paprika (if using) together in a small bowl. Rub it all over the pork.
3. In a medium bowl, toss the Brussels sprouts and onion with the oil, maple syrup, and rosemary. Spoon the mixture around the pork.
4. Roast the pork and Brussels sprouts until the pork is brown outside and slightly pink inside (internal temperature should be 145°F). Remove from the oven and let rest for 3 minutes.
5. Divide the vegetables evenly among four plates. Slice the pork into 1½-inch-thick pieces and top each plate with three or four pieces.

PER SERVING

Calorie 292, Fats 12g, Carbs 15g, Protein 34g

Beef Steak with Shrimps

Prep time: 15 minutes | Cook time: 30 minutes | Serves 2
- 1 tbsp. of butter, melted
- 1 tbsp. of olive oil
- 1 tbsp. of finely minced onion
- 1 tsp. of Worcestershire sauce
- 1 tbsp. of white wine
- 1 tsp. of lemon juice
- 1 tsp. of seafood seasoning
- 1 tsp. of dried parsley
- 1 clove of garlic, minced
- 12 shrimp (medium), peeled & deveined
- ⅛ tsp. of black pepper, freshly ground
- 2 filet of mignon steaks (4 ounce)
- 1 tsp. of steak seasoning
- 2 tsp. of olive oil

1. In a bowl, combine shrimp with 1 tbsp. oil, onion, butter, wine, lemon juice, Worcestershire sauce, parsley, garlic, seafood seasoning, and black pepper. Evenly coat by tossing. Refrigerate for at least 15-20 minutes to let flavors meld before removing plastic wrap from the bowl.
2. Set an outside grill over medium-high heat and give the grates quick oiling. Two teaspoons of olive oil and steak seasoning should be applied to the steaks.
3. Cook steaks for 5 to 7 minutes on each side, or until they are starting to firm up and are the appropriate degree of doneness. The inside temperature should register 140 degrees Fahrenheit on an instant-read thermometer (60 degrees C). Place the steaks on a plate and cover them loosely with a sheet of aluminum foil.
4. Remove shrimp from the marinade and grill for two to three minutes on each side, or until the shrimp are brilliant pink on the exterior and the flesh is no longer translucent.

PER SERVING

Total Calories: 444kcal, Fats: 35.2g, Carbohydrates: 2.7g, Protein: 26.9g, Fiber: 0.3g, Sodium: 925.6mg, Potassium: 385.3mg ..

Easy Beef Kofta

Prep time: 10 minutes | Cook time:10 minutes | Serves 6
- 2 lbs. ground beef
- 4 garlic cloves, minced
- 1 onion, minced
- 2 teaspoon cumin
- 1 cup fresh parsley, chopped
- ¼ teaspoon pepper
- 1 teaspoon salt
- 1 tablespoon oil
1. With a knife, chop the beef very well.
2. Add the rest of the ingredients excluding oil into the mixing bowl and mix until combined.
3. Roll meat mixture into mini-kebab shapes.
4. Add the oil to a pan then warm up at high flame.
5. Roast the meat in the hot pan for 4-6 minutes on each side or until cooked through.
6. Serve with some vegetables and a sauce as you like.

PER SERVING

Calories 223 Fat 7.3 g Carbohydrates 2.5 g Protein 35 g

Pork Cacciatore

Prep time: 10 minutes | Cook time:2 Hours | Serves 4

- 1 ½ lbs. pork chops
- 1 teaspoon dried oregano
- 1 cup beef broth
- 3 tablespoon tomato paste
- 14 oz. can tomato, diced
- 2 cups mushrooms, sliced
- 1 small onion, diced
- 1 garlic clove, minced
- 2 tablespoon olive oil
- ¼ teaspoon pepper
- ½ teaspoon salt

1. Warmth oil in a pan over medium-high heat.
2. Add pork chops in pan and cook until brown on both the sides.
3. Transfer pork chops into a pot.
4. Pour remaining ingredients over the pork chops.
5. Cover then cook on low flame for 2 hours.
6. Serve and enjoy.

PER SERVING

Calories 440 Fat 33 g Carbohydrates 6 g Protein 28 g ..

Pork Roast

Prep time: 10 minutes | Cook time:1 hour 35 minutes | Serves 6

- 3 lbs. pork roast, boneless
- 1 cup water
- 1 onion, chopped
- 3 garlic cloves, chopped
- 1 tablespoon black pepper
- 1 rosemary sprig
- 2 fresh oregano sprigs
- 2 fresh thyme sprigs
- 1 tablespoon olive oil
- 1 tablespoon kosher salt

1. Preheat the oven to 350 F.
2. Season pork roast with pepper and salt.
3. Heat olive oil in an oven-proof stockpot and sear pork roast on all sides, about 4 to 6 minutes.
4. Add onion and garlic. Pour in the water, rosemary, oregano, and thyme and bring to boil for a minute.
5. Cover pot and roast in the preheated oven for 1 1/2 hours.
6. Serve and enjoy.

PER SERVING

Calories 502 Fat 23.8 g Carbohydrates 3 g Protein 65 g

Greek Pork Chops

Prep time: 10 minutes | Cook time:15 minutes | Serves 4

- 8 pork chops, boneless
- 4 teaspoon dried oregano
- 2 tablespoon Worcestershire sauce
- 3 tablespoon fresh lemon juice
- ¼ cup olive oil
- 1 teaspoon ground mustard
- 2 teaspoon garlic powder
- 2 teaspoon onion powder
- Pepper
- Salt

1. Whisk together oil, garlic powder, onion powder, oregano, Worcestershire sauce, lemon juice, mustard, pepper, and salt.
2. Place pork chops in a baking dish then pour marinade over pork chops and coat well. Place in refrigerator overnight.
3. Preheat the grill.
4. Place pork chops on hot grill and cook for 7-8 minutes on each side.
5. Serve and enjoy.

PER SERVING

Calories 324 Fat 26.5 g Carbohydrates 2.5 g Sugar 1.3 g Protein 18 g Cholesterol 69 mg ..

Pork Chops alla Pizzaiola

Prep time: 15 minutes | Cook time: 20 minutes| Serves 4

- 1 (15-oz) can diced tomatoes, in juice
- 1 tsp herbes de provence
- ¼ tsp dried red pepper flakes, or more to taste
- 1 Tbsp chopped fresh Italian parsley leaves

1. In a heavy large skillet, heat the oil over medium heat. Sprinkle the pork chops with salt and pepper.
2. Add the pork chops to the skillet and cook until they are brown and an instant-read meat thermometer inserted horizontally into the pork registers 160°F, about 3 minutes per side.
3. Transfer the pork chops to a plate and tent with foil to keep them warm.
4. Add the onion to the same skillet and sauté over medium heat until crisp-tender, about 4 minutes.
5. Add the tomatoes with their juices, herbes de Provence, and 1/4 teaspoon red pepper flakes. Cover and simmer until the flavors blend and the juices thicken slightly, stirring occasionally, about 15 minutes. Season the sauce, to taste, with salt and more red pepper flakes. Return the pork chops and any accumulated juices from the plate to the skillet and turn the pork chops to coat with the sauce.
6. Place 1 pork chop on each plate. Spoon the sauce over the pork chops.
7. Sprinkle with the parsley and serve.

PER SERVING

Calorie 341, Fats 22g, Carbs17g, Protein 41g

Seasoned Pork Chops

Prep time: 10 minutes | Cook time: 4 hours | Serves 4

1. 4 pork chops
2. 2 garlic cloves, minced
3. 1 cup chicken broth
4. 1 tablespoon poultry seasoning
5. 1/4 cup olive oil
6. Pepper and salt

7. In a bowl, whisk together olive oil, poultry seasoning, garlic, broth, pepper, and salt.
8. Pour olive oil mixture into the slow cooker then place pork chops in the pot.
9. Cover and cook on low flame for about 3 hours.
10. Uncover the pot and roast at high flame for 10 minutes.
11. Dress the pork in the cooking sauce and serve along with vegetables.

PER SERVING

Calories 386 Fat 32.9 g Carbohydrates 3 g Protein 20 g

Perfectly Grilled Steak

Prep time: 15 minutes | Cook time: 30 minutes | Serves 4

- 2 tablespoons canola or extra-virgin olive oil
- 4 1 1/4-to-1 1/2-inch-thick boneless rib-eye or New York strip steaks
- Kosher salt and freshly ground pepper

1. Remove the steaks from the refrigerator about 20 minutes before grilling and let sit, covered, at room temperature.
2. Heat your grill to high. Brush the steaks on both sides with oil and season liberally with salt and pepper.
3. Place the steaks on the grill and cook for 5 minutes or until golden brown and slightly charred.
4. Turn the steaks over and continue to grill 3 to 5 minutes for medium-rare (an internal temperature of 135 degrees F), 5 to 7 minutes for medium (140 degrees F) or 8 to 10 minutes for medium-well (150 degrees F).
5. Transfer the steaks to a cutting board or platter, tent loosely with foil and let rest 5 minutes before slicing.

PER SERVING

Calorie 341, Fats 22g, Carbs17g, Protein 41g.

Chapter 9
Fish & Seafoods

Fast Seafood Paella

Prep time: 15 minutes| Cook time: 20 minutes| Serves 4

- ¼ cup plus 1 tablespoon extra-virgin olive oil
- 1 large onion, finely chopped
- 2 tomatoes, peeled and chopped
- 1½ tablespoons garlic powder
- 1½ cups medium-grain Spanish paella rice or arborio rice
- 2 carrots, finely diced
- Salt, to taste
- 1 tablespoon sweet paprika
- 8 ounces (227 g) lobster meat or canned crab
- ½ cup frozen peas
- 3 cups chicken stock, plus more if needed
- 1 cup dry white wine
- 6 jumbo shrimp, unpeeled
- 1/3 pound (136 g) calamari rings
- 1 lemon, halved

1. In a large sauté pan or skillet (16-inch is ideal), heat the oil over medium heat until small bubbles start to escape from oil.
2. Add the onion and cook for about 3 minutes, until fragrant, then add tomatoes and garlic powder. Cook for 5 to 10 minutes, until the tomatoes are reduced by half and the consistency is sticky.
3. Stir in the rice, carrots, salt, paprika, lobster, and peas and mix well. In a pot or microwave-safe bowl, heat the chicken stock to almost boiling, then add it to the rice mixture. Bring to a simmer, then add the wine.
4. Smooth out the rice in the bottom of the pan. Cover and cook on low for 10 minutes, mixing occasionally, to prevent burning.
5. Top the rice with the shrimp, cover, and cook for 5 more minutes. Add additional broth to the pan if the rice looks dried out.
6. Right before removing the skillet from the heat, add the calamari rings. Toss the ingredients frequently.
7. In about 2 minutes, the rings will look opaque. Remove the pan from the heat immediately—you don't want the paella to overcook). Squeeze fresh lemon juice over the dish.

PER SERVING

Calories: 632 Fat: 20g Protein: 34g Carbs: 71g

Crispy Fried Sardines

Prep time: 15 minutes| Cook time: 5 minutes| Serves 4

- avocado oil, as needed
- 1½ pounds (680 g) whole fresh sardines, scales removed
- 1 teaspoon salt
- 1 teaspoon freshly ground black pepper
- 2 cups flour

1. Preheat a deep skillet over medium heat. Pour in enough oil so there is about 1 inch of it in the pan. Season the fish with the salt and pepper.

2. Dredge the fish in the flour so it is completely covered. Slowly drop in 1 fish at a time, making sure not to overcrowd the pan.
3. Cook for about 3 minutes on each side or just until the fish begins to brown on all sides. Serve warm.

PER SERVING

Calories: 794 Fat: 47g Protein: 48g Carbs: 44g

Orange Roasted Salmon

Prep time: 15 minutes| Cook time: 25 minutes| Serves 4

- ½ cup extra-virgin olive oil, divided
- 2 tablespoons balsamic vinegar
- 2 tablespoons garlic powder, divided
- 1 tablespoon cumin seeds
- 1 teaspoon sea salt, divided
- 1 teaspoon freshly ground black pepper, divided
- 2 teaspoons smoked paprika
- 4 (8-ounce / 227-g) wild salmon fillets, skinless
- 2 small red onions, thinly sliced
- ½ cup halved Campari tomatoes
- 1 small fennel bulb, thinly sliced lengthwise
- 1 large carrot, thinly sliced
- 8 medium portobello mushrooms
- 8 medium radishes, sliced 1/8 inch thick
- ½ cup dry white wine
- ½ lime, zested
- Handful cilantro leaves
- ½ cup halved pitted Kalamata olives
- 1 orange, thinly sliced
- 4 roasted sweet potatoes, cut in wedges lengthwise

1. Preheat the oven to 375°f (190°c). In a medium bowl, mix 6 tablespoons of olive oil, the balsamic vinegar, 1 tablespoon of garlic powder, the cumin seeds, ¼ teaspoon of sea salt, ¼ teaspoon of pepper, and the paprika.
2. Put the salmon in the bowl and marinate while preparing the vegetables, about 10 minutes.
3. Heat an oven-safe sauté pan or skillet on medium-high heat and sear the top of the salmon for about 2 minutes, or until lightly brown. Set aside.
4. Add the remaining 2 tablespoons of olive oil to the same skillet. Once it's hot, add the onion, tomatoes, fennel, carrot, mushrooms, radishes, the remaining 1 teaspoon of garlic powder, ¾ teaspoon of salt, and ¾ teaspoon of pepper.
5. Mix well and cook for 5 to 7 minutes, until fragrant. Add wine and mix well. Place the salmon on top of the vegetable mixture, browned-side up.
6. Sprinkle the fish with lime zest and cilantro and place the olives around the fish. Put orange slices over the fish and cook for about 7 additional minutes.
7. While this is baking, add the sliced sweet potato wedges on a baking sheet and bake this alongside the skillet. Remove from the oven, cover the skillet tightly, and let rest for about 3 minutes.

PER SERVING

Calories: 841 Fat: 41g Protein: 59g Carbs: 60g

Lemon Rosemary Branzino

Prep time: 15 minutes| Cook time: 30 minutes| Serves 4

- 4 tablespoons extra-virgin olive oil, divided
- 2 (8-ounce / 227-g) branzino fillets, preferably at least 1 inch thick
- 1 garlic clove, minced
- 1 bunch scallions, white part only, thinly sliced
- ½ cup sliced pitted Kalamata or other good-quality black olives
- 1 large carrot, cut into ¼-inch rounds
- 10 to 12 small cherry tomatoes, halved
- ½ cup dry white wine
- 2 tablespoons paprika
- 2 teaspoons kosher salt
- ½ tablespoon ground chili pepper, preferably Turkish or Aleppo
- 2 rosemary sprigs or 1 tablespoon dried rosemary
- 1 small lemon, very thinly sliced

1. Warm a large, oven-safe sauté pan or skillet over high heat until hot, about 2 minutes. Carefully add 1 tablespoon of olive oil and heat until it shimmers, 10 to 15 seconds.
2. Brown the branzino fillets for 2 minutes, skin-side up. Carefully flip the fillets skin-side down and cook for another 2 minutes, until browned. Set aside.
3. Swirl 2 tablespoons of olive oil around the skillet to coat evenly. Add the garlic, scallions, kalamata olives, carrot, and tomatoes, and let the vegetables sauté for 5 minutes, until softened.
4. Add the wine, stirring until all ingredients are well integrated. Carefully place the fish over the sauce. Preheat the oven to 450°f (235°c).
5. While the oven is heating, brush the fillets with 1 tablespoon of olive oil and season with paprika, salt, and chili pepper.
6. Top each fillet with a rosemary sprig and several slices of lemon. Scatter the olives over fish and around the pan. Roast until lemon slices are browned or singed, about 10 minutes.

PER SERVING

Calories: 725 fats: 43g protein: 58g carbs: 25g

Almond-Crusted Swordfish

Prep time: 15 minutes| Cook time: 15 minutes| Serves 4

- ½ cup almond flour
- ¼ cup crushed Marcona almonds
- ½ to 1 teaspoon salt, divided
- 2 pounds (907 g) Swordfish, preferably 1 inch thick
- 1 large egg, beaten (optional)
- ¼ cup pure apple cider
- ¼ cup extra-virgin olive oil, plus more for frying
- 3 to 4 sprigs flat-leaf parsley, chopped
- 1 lemon, juiced
- 1 tablespoon Spanish paprika
- 5 medium baby portobello mushrooms, chopped (optional)
- 4 or 5 chopped scallions, both green and white parts
- 3 to 4 garlic cloves, peeled
- ¼ cup chopped pitted Kalamata olives

1. On a dinner plate, spread the flour and crushed Marcona almonds and mix in the salt. Alternately, pour the flour, almonds, and ¼ teaspoon of salt into a large plastic food storage bag.
2. Add the fish and coat it with the flour mixture. If a thicker coat is desired, repeat this step after dipping the fish in the egg (if using).
3. In a measuring cup, combine the apple cider, ¼ cup of olive oil, parsley, lemon juice, paprika, and ¼ teaspoon of salt. Mix well and set aside.
4. In a large, heavy-bottom sauté pan or skillet, pour the olive oil to a depth of ⅛ inch and heat on medium heat.
5. Once the oil is hot, add the fish and brown for 3 to 5 minutes, then turn the fish over and add the mushrooms (If using), scallions, garlic, and olives.
6. Cook for an additional 3 minutes. Once the other side of the fish is brown, remove the fish from the pan and set aside.
7. Pour the cider mixture into the skillet and mix well with the vegetables. Put the fried fish into the skillet on top of the mixture and cook with sauce on medium-low heat for 10 minutes, until the fish flakes easily with a fork.
8. Carefully remove the fish from the pan and plate. Spoon the sauce over the fish. Serve with white rice or home-fried potatoes.

PER SERVING

Calories: 620 Fat: 37g Protein: 63g Carbs: 10g

Sea Bass Crusted with Moroccan Spices

Prep time: 15 minutes| Cook time: 40 minutes| Serves 4

- 1½ teaspoons ground turmeric, divided
- ¾ teaspoon saffron
- ½ teaspoon ground cumin
- ¼ teaspoon kosher salt
- ¼ teaspoon freshly ground black pepper
- 1½ pounds (680 g) sea bass fillets, about ½ inch thick
- 8 tablespoons extra-virgin olive oil, divided
- 8 garlic cloves, divided (4 minced cloves and 4 sliced)
- 6 medium baby portobello mushrooms, chopped
- 1 large carrot, sliced on an angle
- 2 sun-dried tomatoes, thinly sliced (optional)
- 2 tablespoons tomato paste
- 1 (15-ounce / 425-g) can chickpeas, drained and rinsed
- 1½ cups low-sodium vegetable broth
- ¼ cup white wine
- 1 tablespoon ground coriander (optional)
- 1 cup sliced artichoke hearts marinated in olive oil
- ½ cup pitted Kalamata olives
- ½ lemon, juiced
- ½ lemon, cut into thin rounds
- 4 to 5 rosemary sprigs or 2 tablespoons dried rosemary
- Fresh cilantro, for garnish

1. In a small mixing bowl, combine 1 teaspoon turmeric and the saffron and cumin. Season with salt and pepper. Season both sides of the fish with the spice mixture.
2. Add 3 tablespoons of olive oil and work the fish to make sure it's well coated with the spices and the olive oil.
3. In a large sauté pan or skillet, heat 2 tablespoons of olive oil over medium heat until shimmering but not smoking. Sear the top side of the sea bass for about 1 minute, or until golden. Remove and set aside.
4. In the same skillet, add the minced garlic and cook very briefly, tossing regularly, until fragrant. Add the mushrooms, carrot, sun-dried tomatoes (if using), and tomato paste.
5. Cook for 3 to 4 minutes over medium heat, tossing frequently, until fragrant. Add the chickpeas, broth, wine, coriander (if using), and the sliced garlic.
6. Stir in the remaining ½ teaspoon ground turmeric. Raise the heat, if needed, and bring to a boil, then lower heat to simmer. Cover part of the way and let the sauce simmer for about 20 minutes, until thickened.
7. Carefully add the seared fish to the skillet. Ladle a bit of the sauce on top of the fish. Add the artichokes, olives, lemon juice and slices, and rosemary sprigs.
8. Cook another 10 minutes or until the fish is fully cooked and flaky. Garnish with fresh cilantro.

PER SERVING

Calories: 696 Fat: 41g Protein: 48g Carbs: 37g

Cilantro Lemon Shrimp

Prep time: 20 minutes| Cook time: 10 minutes| Serves 4

- 1/3 cup lemon juice
- 4 garlic cloves
- 1 cup fresh cilantro leaves
- ½ teaspoon ground coriander
- 3 tablespoons extra-virgin olive oil
- 1 teaspoon salt
- 1½ pounds (680 g) large shrimp (21 to 25), deveined and shells removed

1. In a food processor, pulse the lemon juice, garlic, cilantro, coriander, olive oil, and salt 10 times. Put the shrimp in a bowl or plastic zip-top bag, pour in the cilantro marinade, and let sit for 15 minutes.
2. Preheat a skillet on high heat. Put the shrimp and marinade in the skillet. Cook the shrimp for 3 minutes on each side. Serve warm.

PER SERVING

Calories: 225 Fat: 12g Protein: 28g Carbs: 5g

Tasty Grilled Lime Shrimp

Prep time: 10 minutes | Cook time:5 minutes | Serves 4

- 1 pound medium shrimp, peeled and deveined
- 1 lime, juiced
- ½ cup olive oil
- 3 tablespoons Cajun seasoning

1. Take a re-sealable zip bag and add lime juice, Cajun seasoning, and olive oil
2. Add shrimp and shake it well, let it marinate for 20 minutes
3. Preheat your outdoor grill to medium heat
4. Lightly grease the grate
5. Remove shrimp from marinade and cook for 2 minutes per side
6. Serve and enjoy!

PER SERVING

Calories: 188 Fat: 3 g Carbohydrate: 1.2 g Protein: 13 g
Saturated Fat: 1 g Fiber: 0.2 g Sodium: 324 mg

Shrimp with Garlic and Mushrooms

Prep time: 15 minutes| Cook time: 15 minutes| Serves 4

- 1 pound (454 g) peeled and deveined fresh shrimp
- 1 teaspoon salt
- 1 cup extra-virgin olive oil
- 8 large garlic cloves, thinly sliced
- 4 ounces (113 g) sliced mushrooms (shiitake, baby bella, or button)
- ½ teaspoon red pepper flakes
- ¼ cup chopped fresh flat-leaf Italian parsley
- zucchini noodles or riced cauliflower, for serving

1. Rinse the shrimp and pat dry. Place in a small bowl and sprinkle with the salt. In a large rimmed, thick skillet, heat the olive oil over medium-low heat.
2. Add the garlic and heat until very fragrant, 3 to 4 minutes, reducing the heat if the garlic starts to burn.
3. Add the mushrooms and sauté for 5 minutes, until softened. Add the shrimp and red pepper flakes and sauté until the shrimp begins to turn pink, another 3 to 4 minutes.
4. Remove from the heat and stir in the parsley. Serve over zucchini noodles or riced cauliflower.

PER SERVING

Calories: 620 Fat: 56g Protein: 24g Carbs: 4g

Avocado & Salmon Poke Bowl

Prep time: 20 minutes | Cook time: 0 minutes | Serves 4

For Poke:
- ½ cup of yellow onion, thinly sliced
- 1 ripe avocado (medium), diced
- ½ cup of scallion greens, thinly sliced
- ¼ cup of caviar
- ½ cup of fresh cilantro, chopped
- 3 tbsp. of tamari (reduced-sodium)
- ½ tsp. of Sriracha
- 2 tsp. of toasted sesame oil (dark)
- Brown Rice Salad:
- 2 cups of spicy greens (packed), like watercress, arugula, or mizuna
- 2 cups of cooked brown rice (short-grain), warmed
- 2 tbsp. of rice vinegar
- 1 tbsp. of Dijon mustard or Chinese-style
- 2 tbsp. of olive oil

1. Salmon, onion, avocado, scallion greens, caviar, cilantro, tamari, sesame oil, & Sriracha should all be gently mixed together in a medium bowl.
2. In a big bowl, mix the greens and the rice. In a small bowl, combine the oil, mustard, and vinegar. Add to rice salad and well combine. Serve the rice salad with the poke.

PER SERVING

Total Calories: 442kcal, Fats: 21.9g, Carbohydrates: 34.3g, Protein: 29.5g, Fiber: 7g, Sodium: 791.7mg, Potassium: 828mg

Pistachio-Crusted Whitefish

Prep time: 10 minutes | Cook time: 20 minutes | Serves 2

- ¼ cup shelled pistachios
- 1 tablespoon fresh parsley
- 1 tablespoon panko bread crumbs
- 2 tablespoons olive oil
- ¼ teaspoon salt
- 10 ounces' skinless whitefish (1 large piece or 2 smaller ones)

1. Preheat the oven to 350°F and set the rack to the middle position. Line a sheet pan with foil or parchment paper.
2. Combine all of the ingredients except the fish in a mini food processor, and pulse until the nuts are finely ground.
3. Alternatively, you can mince the nuts with a chef's knife and combine the ingredients by hand in a small bowl.
4. Place the fish on the sheet pan. Spread the nut mixture evenly over the fish and pat it down lightly.
5. Bake the fish for 20 to 30 minutes, depending on the thickness, until it flakes easily with a fork.
6. Keep in mind that a thicker cut of fish takes a bit longer to bake. You'll know it's done when it's opaque, flakes apart easily with a fork, or reaches an internal temperature of 145°F.

PER SERVING

Calories: 185, Carbs - 23.8 g, Protein - 10.1 g, Fat - 5.2 g

Seafood Risotto

Prep time: 15 minutes| Cook time: 30 minutes| Serves 4
- 6 cups vegetable broth
- 3 tablespoons extra-virgin olive oil
- 1 large onion, chopped
- 3 cloves garlic, minced
- ½ teaspoon saffron threads
- 1½ cups arborio rice
- 1½ teaspoons salt
- 8 ounces (227 g) shrimp (21 to 25), peeled and deveined
- 8 ounces (227 g) scallops

1. In a large saucepan over medium heat, bring the broth to a low simmer. In a large skillet over medium heat, cook the olive oil, onion, garlic, and saffron for 3 minutes.
2. Add the rice, salt, and 1 cup of the broth to the skillet. Stir the ingredients together and cook over low heat until most of the liquid is absorbed.
3. Repeat steps with broth, adding ½ cup of broth at a time, and cook until all but ½ cup of the broth is absorbed.
4. Add the shrimp and scallops when you stir in the final ½ cup of broth. Cover and let cook for 10 minutes. Serve warm.

PER SERVING

Calories: 460 Fat: 12g Protein: 24g Carbs: 64g

Crispy Homemade Fish Sticks Recipe

Prep time: 10 minutes | Cook time: 15 minutes | Serves 2

- ½ cup of flour
- 1 beaten egg
- 1 cup of flour
- ½ cup of bread crumbs.
- Zest of 1 lemon juice
- Parsley
- Salt
- 1 teaspoon of black pepper
- 1 tablespoon of sweet paprika
- 1 teaspoon of oregano
- 1½ lb. of wild salmon
- Extra virgin olive oil

1. Preheat your oven to about 450 degrees F. Get a bowl, dry your salmon and season its two sides with the salt.
2. Then chop into small sizes of 1½ inch length each. Get a bowl and mix black pepper with oregano.
3. Add paprika to the mixture and blend it. Then spice the fish stick with the mixture you have just made. Get another dish and pour your flours.
4. You will need a different bowl again to pour your egg wash into. Pick yet the fourth dish, mix your breadcrumb with your cheese and add lemon zest to the mixture.
5. Return to the fish sticks and dip each fish into flour such that both sides are coated with flour. As you dip each fish into flour, take it out and dip it into egg wash and lastly, dip it in the breadcrumb mixture.
6. Do this for all fish sticks and arrange on a baking sheet. Ensure you oil the baking sheet before arranging the stick thereon and drizzle the top of the fish sticks with extra virgin olive oil.
7. Caution: allow excess flours to fall off a fish before dipping it into other ingredients.
8. Also ensure that you do not let the coating peel while you add extra virgin olive oil on top of the fishes.
9. Fix the baking sheet in the middle of the oven and allow it to cook for 13 min. By then, the fishes should be golden brown and you can collect them from the oven, and you can serve immediately.
10. Top it with your lemon zest, parsley and fresh lemon juice.

PER SERVING

Calories: 119 fat3.4g sodium 293mg carbs 9.3g protein 13.5g protein

Sauced Shellfish in White Wine

Prep time: 10 minutes | Cook time: 10 minutes | Serves 2

- 2-lbs fresh cuttlefish
- ½-cup olive oil
- 1-pc large onion, finely chopped
- 1-cup of Robola white wine
- ¼-cup lukewarm water
- 1-pc bay leaf
- ½-bunch parsley, chopped
- 4-pcs tomatoes, grated
- Salt and pepper

1. Take out the hard centerpiece of cartilage (cuttlebone), the bag of ink, and the intestines from the cuttlefish.
2. Wash the cleaned cuttlefish with running water. Slice it into small pieces, and drain excess water.
3. Heat the oil in a saucepan placed over medium-high heat and sauté the onion for 3 minutes until tender.
4. Add the sliced cuttlefish and pour in the white wine. Cook for 5 minutes until it simmers.
5. Pour in the water, and add the tomatoes, bay leaf, parsley, tomatoes, salt, and pepper. Simmer the mixture over low heat until the cuttlefish slices are tender and left with their thick sauce. Serve them warm with rice.
6. Be careful not to overcook the cuttlefish as its texture becomes very hard. A safe rule of thumb is grilling the cuttlefish over a ragingly hot fire for 3 minutes before using it in any recipe.

PER SERVING

Calories: 308, Fats: 18.1g, Dietary Fiber: 1.5g, Carbs: 8g, Protein: 25.6g

Baked Salmon & Black Rice

Prep time: 10 minutes | Cook time: 50 minutes | Serves 3

- 1 cup of black rice
- 3 salmon fillets (4 oz. each)
- 2 cups of water
- 3 tbsp. of dried cranberries
- ½ cup of sugar snap peas
- 1 tsp. of garlic powder
- ¼ tsp. of pepper
- ½ tsp. of salt
- 1 tbsp. of orange zest

1. To make rice, combine 1 cup of black rice with 2 cups of water in a rice cooker. OR cook the rice and salt in 2 cups of water on the stovetop. Cook rice on low for 30 to 35 minutes, or until it is soft.
2. Turn the oven on to 400 degrees. Add salt, pepper, and garlic to the fish. Put the item onto a baking sheet and bake for 15 to 20 minutes.
3. As soon as the rice is finished cooking, stir in the snap peas, salt, cranberries, and pepper. Add salmon and orange zest to the top. To taste, add salt and pepper. Rosemary is a nice garnish. (optional)

PER SERVING

Total Calories: 288kcal, Fats: 2g, Carbohydrates: 62g, Protein: 5g, Fiber: 3g, Sodium: 402mg, Potassium: 182mg

Pistachio Sole Fish

Prep time: 5 minutes | Cook time: 10 minutes | Serves 2

- 4 (5 ounces) boneless sole fillets
- ½ cup pistachios, finely chopped
- Juice of 1 lemon
- Teaspoon extra virgin olive oil

1. Pre-heat your oven to 350 degrees Fahrenheit
2. Wrap baking sheet using parchment paper and keep it on the side
3. Pat fish dry with kitchen towels and lightly season with salt and pepper
4. Take a small bowl and stir in pistachios
5. Place sol on the prepped sheet and press 2 tablespoons of pistachio mixture on top of each fillet
6. Rub the fish with lemon juice and olive oil
7. Bake for 10 minutes until the top is golden and fish flakes with a fork.

PER SERVING

Calories: 166 Fat 6g Carbs2g

Speedy Tilapia with Red Onion and Avocado

Prep time: 10 minutes| Cook time: 5 minutes| Serves 2

- 1 tablespoon extra-virgin olive oil
- 1 tablespoon freshly squeezed orange juice
- ¼ teaspoon kosher or sea salt
- 4 (4-ounces) tilapia fillets, more oblong than square, skin-on or skinned
- ¼ cup chopped red onion (about 1/8 onion)
- 1 avocado, pitted, skinned, and sliced

1. In a 9-inch glass pie dish, use a fork to mix together the oil, orange juice, and salt. Working with one fillet at a time, place each in the pie dish and turn to coat on all sides.
2. Arrange the fillets in a wagon-wheel formation, so that one end of each fillet is in the center of the dish and the other end is temporarily draped over the edge of the dish.
3. Top each fillet with 1 tablespoon of onion, then fold the end of the fillet that's hanging over the edge in half over the onion.
4. When finished, you should have 4 folded-over fillets with the fold against the outer edge of the dish and the ends all in the center.
5. Cover the dish with plastic wrap, leaving a small part open at the edge to vent the steam. Microwave on high for about 3 minutes.
6. The fish is done when it just begins to separate into flakes (chunks) when pressed gently with a fork. Top the fillets with the avocado and serve.

PER SERVING

Carbs 4g fiber3g protein22g

Tasty Coconut and Hazelnut Haddock

Prep time: 10 minutes | Cook time:12 minutes | Serves 4

- 4 haddock fillets, 5 ounces each, boneless
- 2 tablespoons coconut oil,
- 1 cup coconut, shredded and unsweetened
- ¼ cup hazelnuts, ground
- Salt to taste
- Some cooked spinach

1. Preheat your oven to 400 degrees F
2. Line a baking sheet with parchment paper
3. Keep it on the side
4. Pat fish fillets dry with a paper towel and season with salt
5. Take a bowl and stir in the hazelnuts and shredded coconut
6. Drag fish fillets through the coconut mix until both sides are coated well
7. Transfer to the baking sheet
8. Brush with coconut oil
9. Bake for about 12 minutes until flaky
10. Serve over a bed of cooked spinach and enjoy!

PER SERVING

Calories: 300 Fat: 24 g Carbohydrate: 1 g Protein: 20 g Saturated Fat: 4 g Fiber: 0.2 g Sodium: 400 mg

The Definitive Calamari

Prep time: 10 minutes | Cook time:8 minutes | Serves 4

- 2 tablespoons extra virgin olive oil
- 1 teaspoon chili powder
- ½ teaspoon ground cumin
- Zest of 1 lime
- Juice of 1 lime
- Dash of sea salt
- 1 and ½ pounds squid, cleaned and split open, with tentacles cut into ½ inch rounds
- 2 tablespoons cilantro, chopped
- 2 tablespoons red bell pepper, minced

1. Take a medium bowl and stir in olive oil, chili powder, cumin, lime zest, sea salt, lime juice, and pepper
2. Add squid, stir to coat, and let it marinade in the refrigerator for 1 hour
3. Preheat your oven to broil
4. Arrange squid on a baking sheet, broil for 8 minutes turn once until tender
5. Garnish the broiled calamari with cilantro and red bell pepper
6. Serve and enjoy!

PER SERVING

Calories: 159 Fat: 13 g Saturated Fat: 3 g Carbohydrates: 12 g Fiber: 3 g Sodium: 412 mg Protein: 3 g

Oil-Poached Whitefish with Lemony Gremolata

Prep time: 1 hour 10 minutes | Cook time:15 minutes | Serves 4

- 2(¾ pound) whitefish fillets, skinless, Arctic char, or similar
- 1 teaspoon kosher salt
- 1 teaspoon freshly ground black pepper
- ½ cup extra-virgin olive oil
- 3 cloves garlic, minced
- 3/4 cup fresh parsley leaves, minced, divided
- ¼ cup lemon zest, grated, divided

1. Place the fish fillets lengthwise in a 13-by-9-inch baking dish
2. Season with salt and pepper on both sides
3. Take a small bowl, whisk together the olive oil, garlic, half of the parsley, and half of the lemon zest
4. Pour the mixture evenly over the fish, cover, and marinate in the refrigerator for at least 1 hour and up to overnight.
5. Preheat your oven to 350 degrees F
6. Bake the fish for 15 to 20 minutes
7. Cut each fillet into 2 pieces, top evenly with the remaining parsley and lemon zest
8. Serve with lemony Sautéed Chard with Red Onion and Herbs or any other vegetable side or salad
9. Serve and enjoy!

PER SERVING

Calories: 535 Fat: 28 g Carbohydrate: 3 g Protein: 37 g Saturated Fat: 10g Fiber: 1 g Sodium: 622 mg

Shrimp Scampi with Baby Spinach

Prep time: 10 minutes | Cook time:10 minutes | Serves 4

- 1 pound jumbo shrimp (about 12), peeled and deveined
- 6 to 8 cups (6 ounces) baby spinach leaves
- 1 cup unsalted chicken broth or stock
- 3 tablespoons extra-virgin olive oil, divided
- 6 cloves garlic, minced
- Grated zest and juice from 1 medium lemon
- ¼ cup (½ stick) cold unsalted grass-fed butter, cubed

- ¼ teaspoon sea salt or Himalayan salt, or to taste
- ½ teaspoon red pepper flakes, or to taste
- ½ teaspoon freshly ground black pepper, or to taste
- 2 to 3 tablespoons chopped fresh parsley, optional

1. Pat the shrimp very dry with paper towels
2. Take a large skillet and add 2 tablespoons olive oil
3. Heat over medium-high heat
4. Add the shrimp and cook until pink, flipping once, about 2 minutes per side. Remove with a slotted spoon and set aside
5. Reduce the heat to medium and add the remaining 1 tablespoon oil
6. Add the garlic and cook until just fragrant, about 1 minute
7. Add the broth, lemon zest and juice, red pepper flakes, salt, and black pepper, increase the heat to medium-high, and bring to a simmer
8. Reduce the sauce by half, scraping up any browned bits from the bottom with a wooden spoon, about 5 minutes
9. Remove the pan from the heat and allow it to cool slightly
10. Add butter, one cube at a time, stirring continually with a wooden spoon until the sauce thickens
11. Top each plate with about 4 shrimp and divide the sauce evenly among the plates and garnish with the parsley
12. Serve and enjoy!

PER SERVING

Calories: 644 Fat: 46 g Carbohydrate: 9 g Protein: 53 g Saturated Fat: 17g Fiber: 2 g Sodium: 826 mg

Walnut Encrusted Salmon

Prep time: 10 minutes | Cook time:15 minutes | Serves 4

- ½ cup walnuts
- 2 tablespoons stevia
- ½ tablespoon Dijon mustard
- ¼ teaspoon dill
- 2 salmon fillets (3 ounces each)
- 1 tablespoon olive oil
- Salt and pepper to taste

1. Preheat your oven to 350 degrees F
2. Add walnuts, mustard, dill, and stevia to a food processor and process until your desired consistency is achieved
3. Take a frying pan and place it over medium heat
4. Add oil and let it heat up
5. Add salmon, sprinkle with salt and pepper and sear for 3 minutes
6. Cover the fish with the walnut mix and coat well
7. Transfer coated salmon to the baking sheet, bake in the oven for 8 minutes
8. Serve and enjoy!

PER SERVING

Calories: 373 Fat: 43 g Saturated Fat: 10 g Carbohydrates: 4 g Fiber: 2 g Sodium: 158 mg Protein: 20 g

Baked Salmon with Orange Juice

Prep time: 10 minutes | Cook time:10 minutes | Serves 4

- ½ pound salmon steak
- Juice of 1 orange
- Pinch of ginger powder, black pepper, and salt
- Juice of ½ lemon
- 1-ounce coconut milk

1. Rub salmon steak with spices and let it sit for 15 minutes
2. Extract the juice from the orange and lemon and mix the juice well.
3. Pour milk into the mixture and stir
4. Take a baking dish and line it with aluminum foil
5. Place steak on it and pour the sauce over the steak
6. Cover with another sheet of foil and bake for 10 minutes at 350 degrees F
7. Serve and enjoy!

PER SERVING

Calories: 300 Fat: 3 g Saturated Fat: 1 g Carbohydrates: 1 g Fiber: 0.1 g Sodium: 222 mg Protein: 7 g

Italian Salmon Dish

Prep time: 10 minutes | Cook time:6 minutes | Serves 4

- ¾ cup of water
- Few sprigs of parsley, basil, tarragon, basil
- 1 pound of salmon, skin on
- 3 teaspoon of ghee
- ¼ teaspoon of salt
- ½ teaspoon of pepper
- ½ a lemon, thinly sliced
- 1 whole carrot, julienned

1. Set your pressure pot to Sauté mode and add the water and herbs
2. Place a steamer rack inside your pot and place salmon on it
3. Drizzle Ghee over the salmon and season with salt and pepper
4. Cover the fish with lemon slices
5. Lock up the lid and cook on HIGH pressure for 3 minutes
6. Release the pressure naturally over 10 minutes
7. Transfer the salmon to a serving platter
8. Set your pot to Sauté mode and add vegetables
9. Cook for 1-2 minutes
10. Serve the salmon with the vegetables
11. Enjoy!

PER SERVING

Calories: 464 Fat: 34 g Saturated Fat: 7 g Carbohydrates: 3 g Fiber: 1 g Sodium: 355 mg Protein: 15 g

Orange and Garlic Shrimp

Prep time: 10 minutes | Cook time:20 minutes | Serves 5

- 1 large orange
- 3 tablespoons extra-virgin olive oil, divided
- 1 tablespoon chopped fresh rosemary
- 1 tablespoon chopped fresh thyme (about 6 sprigs) or 1 teaspoon dried thyme
- 3 garlic cloves, minced (about 11/2 teaspoons)
- 1/4 teaspoon freshly ground black pepper
- 1/4 teaspoon kosher or sea salt
- 1 1/2 pounds fresh raw shrimp, (or frozen and thawed raw shrimp) shells and tails removed

1. Zest the entire orange using a Micro plane or citrus grater.
2. Using a zip-top bag, mix the orange zest and 2 tablespoons of oil with the rosemary, thyme, garlic, pepper, and salt. Add the shrimp, seal the bag, and gently massage the shrimp.
3. Heat a grill, grill pan, or a large skillet over medium heat. Brush on or swirl in the remaining 1 tablespoon of oil. Add half the shrimp, and cook for 4 to 6 minutes, or until the shrimp turn pink, flipping halfway through if on the grill or stirring every minute if in a pan.
4. While the shrimp is cooking, peel the orange and cut the flesh into bite-size pieces. Serve immediately with the shrimp or refrigerate and serve cold.

PER SERVING

Calories: 223 Total Fat: 7g Saturated Fat: 10g Cholesterol: 45 Sodium: =15mg Total Carbohydrates: 8g Fiber: 3g; Protein: 6g

Roasted Shrimp-Gnocchi Bake

Prep time: 10 minutes | Cook time:20 minutes | Serves 6

- 1 cup tomato
- 2 tablespoons extra-virgin olive oil
- 2 garlic cloves, minced
- 1/2 teaspoon black pepper
- 1/4 teaspoon crushed red pepper
- 1 jar roasted red peppers
- 1-pound fresh raw shrimp peeled and deveined
- 1-pound frozen gnocchi
- 1/2 cup cubed feta cheese
- 1/3 cup fresh torn basil leaves

1. Preheat the oven to 425°F.
2. In a baking dish, mix the tomatoes, oil, garlic, black pepper, and crushed red pepper. Roast in the oven for 10 minutes.
3. Stir in the roasted peppers and shrimp. Roast for 10 more minutes, until the shrimp turn pink and white.
4. While the shrimp cooks, cook the gnocchi on the stove top according to the package directions. Drain in a colander and keep warm.
5. Remove the dish from the oven. Mix in the cooked gnocchi, feta, and basil, and serve.

PER SERVING

Calories: 223 Total Fat: 7g Saturated Fat: 16g Cholesterol: 25 Sodium: =10mg Total Carbohydrates: 8g Fiber: 3g; Protein: 6g

Spicy Shrimp Puttanesca

Prep time:5 minutes | Cook time:15 minutes | Serves 4

- 2 tablespoons extra-virgin olive oil
- 3 anchovy fillets, drained and chopped (half a 2-ounce tin), or 1 1/2 teaspoons anchovy paste
- 3 garlic cloves, minced (about 1 1/2 teaspoons)
- 1/2 teaspoon crushed red pepper
- 1 (14.5-ounce) can low-sodium or no-salt-added diced tomatoes, untrained
- 1 (2.25-ounce) can sliced black olives, drained (about 1/2 cup)
- 2 tablespoons capers
- 1 tablespoon chopped fresh oregano or 1 teaspoon dried oregano
- 1-pound fresh raw shrimp (or frozen and thawed shrimp), shells and tails removed

1. In a large skillet over medium heat, heat the oil. Mix in the anchovies, garlic, and crushed red pepper. Cook for 3 minutes, stirring frequently and mashing up the anchovies with a wooden spoon, until they have melted into the oil.
2. Stir in the tomatoes with their juices, olives, capers, and oregano. Turn up the heat to medium-high, and bring to a simmer.
3. When the sauce is lightly bubbling, stir in the shrimp. Reduce the heat, and cook the shrimp until done and serve.

PER SERVING

Calories: 423 Total Fat: 7g Saturated Fat: 16g Cholesterol: 25 Sodium: 55mg Total Carbohydrates: 34g Fiber: 3g; Protein: 6g

Wild Rice, Celery, and Cauliflower Pilaf

Prep time: 15 minutes| Cook time: 45 minutes| Serves 4

- 1 tablespoon olive oil, plus more for greasing the baking dish
- 1 cup wild rice
- 2 cups low-sodium chicken broth
- 1 sweet onion, chopped
- 2 stalks celery, chopped
- 1 teaspoon minced garlic
- 2 carrots, peeled, halved lengthwise, and sliced
- ½ cauliflower head, cut into small florets
- 1 teaspoon chopped fresh thyme
- Sea salt, to taste

1. Preheat the oven to 350°f (180°c). Line a baking sheet with parchment paper and grease with olive oil.
2. Put the wild rice in a saucepan, then pour in the chicken broth. Bring to a boil. Reduce the heat to low and simmer for 30 minutes or until the rice is plump.
3. Meanwhile, heat the remaining olive oil in an oven-proof skillet over medium-high heat until shimmering.
4. Add the onion, celery, and garlic to the skillet and sauté for 3 minutes or until the onion is translucent.
5. Add the carrots and cauliflower to the skillet and sauté for 5 minutes. Turn off the heat and set aside.
6. Pour the cooked rice in the skillet with the vegetables. Sprinkle with thyme and salt. Set the skillet in the preheated oven and bake for 15 minutes or until the vegetables are soft. Serve immediately.

PER SERVING

Calories: 214 Fat: 3.9g Protein: 7.2g Carbs: 37.9g.

Slow Cooked Turkey and Brown Rice

Prep time: 15 minutes| Cook time: 3 hours & 10 minutes| Serves 6

- 1 tablespoon extra-virgin olive oil
- 1½ pounds (680 g) ground turkey
- 2 tablespoons chopped fresh sage, divided
- 2 tablespoons chopped fresh thyme, divided
- 1 teaspoon sea salt
- ½ teaspoon ground black pepper
- 2 cups brown rice
- 1 (14-ounce / 397-g) can stewed tomatoes, with the juice
- ¼ cup pitted and sliced Kalamata olives
- 3 medium zucchinis, sliced thinly
- ¼ cup chopped fresh flat-leaf parsley
- 1 medium yellow onion, chopped
- 1 tablespoon plus 1 teaspoon balsamic vinegar
- 2 cups low-sodium chicken stock
- 2 garlic cloves, minced

1. Heat the olive oil in a nonstick skillet over medium-high heat until shimmering. Add the ground turkey and sprinkle with 1 tablespoon of sage, 1 tablespoon of thyme, salt and ground black pepper.
2. Sauté for 10 minutes or until the ground turkey is lightly browned. Pour them in the slow cooker, then pour in the remaining ingredients. Stir to mix well.
3. Put the lid on and cook on high for 3 hours or until the rice and vegetables are tender. Pour them in a large serving bowl, then spread.

PER SERVING

Calories: 499 Fat: 16.4g Protein: 32.4g Carbs: 56.5g.

Papaya, Jicama, and Peas Rice Bowl

Prep time: 15 minutes| Cook time: 45 minutes| Serves 4

Sauce:
- Juice of ¼ lemon
- 2 teaspoons chopped fresh basil
- 1 tablespoon raw honey
- 1 tablespoon extra-virgin olive oil
- Sea salt, to taste
- Rice:
- 1½ cups wild rice
- 2 papayas, peeled, seeded, and diced
- 1 jicama, peeled and shredded
- 1 cup snow peas, julienned
- 2 cups shredded cabbage
- 1 scallion, white and green parts, chopped

1. Combine the ingredients for the sauce in a bowl. Stir to mix well. Set aside until ready to use. Pour the wild rice in a saucepan, then pour in enough water to cover. Bring to a boil.
2. Reduce the heat to low, then simmer for 45 minutes or until the wild rice is soft and plump. Drain and transfer to a large serving bowl.
3. Top the rice with papayas, jicama, peas, cabbage, and scallion. Pour the sauce over and stir to mix well before serving.

PER SERVING

Calories: 446 Fat: 7.9g Protein: 13.1g Carbs: 85.8g

Italian Baked Beans

Prep time: 5 minutes| Cook time: 15 minutes| Serves 6

- 2 teaspoons extra-virgin olive oil
- ½ cup minced onion (about ¼ onion)
- 1 (12-ounce) can low-sodium tomato paste
- ¼ cup red wine vinegar
- 2 tablespoons honey
- ¼ teaspoon ground cinnamon
- ½ cup water
- 2 (15-ounce) cans cannellini or great northern beans, undrained

1. In a medium saucepan over medium heat, heat the oil. Add the onion and cook for 5 minutes, stirring frequently.
2. Add the tomato paste, vinegar, honey, cinnamon, and water, and mix well. Turn the heat to low. Drain and rinse one can of the beans in a colander and add to the saucepan.
3. Pour the entire second can of beans (including the liquid) into the saucepan. Let it cook for 10 minutes, stirring occasionally, and serve.
4. Ingredient tip: Switch up this recipe by making new variations of the homemade ketchup. Instead of the cinnamon, try ¼ teaspoon of smoked paprika and 1 tablespoon of hot sauce. Serve.

PER SERVING

Calories: 236 Fat: 3g Carbs: 42g Protein: 10g

Cannellini Bean Lettuce Wraps

Prep time: 15 minutes| Cook time: 10 minutes| Serves 4

- 1 tablespoon extra-virgin olive oil
- ½ cup diced red onion (about ¼ onion)
- ¾ cup chopped fresh tomatoes (about 1 medium tomato)
- ¼ teaspoon freshly ground black pepper
- 1 (15-ounce) can cannellini or great northern beans, drained and rinsed
- ¼ cup finely chopped fresh curly parsley
- ½ cup Lemony Garlic Hummus or ½ cup prepared hummus
- 8 romaine lettuce leaves

1. In a large skillet over medium heat, heat the oil. Add the onion and cook for 3 minutes, stirring occasionally.
2. Add the tomatoes and pepper and cook for 3 more minutes, stirring occasionally. Add the beans and cook for 3 more minutes, stirring occasionally. Remove from the heat, and mix in the parsley.
3. Spread 1 tablespoon of hummus over each lettuce leaf. Evenly spread the warm bean mixture down the center of each leaf.
4. Fold one side of the lettuce leaf over the filling lengthwise, then fold over the other side to make a wrap and serve.

PER SERVING

Calories: 211 Fat: 8g Carbs: 28g Protein: 10g..

Israeli Eggplant, Chickpea, and Mint Sauté

Prep time: 5 minutes| Cook time: 20 minutes| Serves 6

- Nonstick cooking spray
- 1 medium globe eggplant (about 1 pound), stem removed
- 1 tablespoon extra-virgin olive oil
- 2 tablespoons freshly squeezed lemon juice (from about 1 small lemon)
- 2 tablespoons balsamic vinegar
- 1 teaspoon ground cumin
- ¼ teaspoon kosher or sea salt
- 1 (15-ounce) can chickpeas, drained and rinsed
- 1 cup sliced sweet onion (about ½ medium Walla Walla or Vidalia onion)
- ¼ cup loosely packed chopped or torn mint leaves
- 1 tablespoon sesame seeds, toasted if desired
- 1 garlic clove, finely minced (about ½ teaspoon)

1. Place one oven rack about 4 inches below the broiler element. Turn the broiler to the highest setting to preheat. Spray a large, rimmed baking sheet with nonstick cooking spray.
2. On a cutting board, cut the eggplant lengthwise into four slabs (each piece should be about ½- to 1/8-inch thick). Place the eggplant slabs on the prepared baking sheet. Set aside.
3. In a small bowl, whisk together the oil, lemon juice, vinegar, cumin, and salt. Brush or drizzle 2 tablespoons of the lemon dressing over both sides of the eggplant slabs. Reserve the remaining dressing.
4. Broil the eggplant directly under the heating element for 4 minutes, flip them, then broil for another 4 minutes, until golden brown.
5. While the eggplant is broiling, in a serving bowl, combine the chickpeas, onion, mint, sesame seeds, and garlic. Add the reserved dressing, and gently mix to incorporate all the ingredients.
6. When the eggplant is done, using tongs, transfer the slabs from the baking sheet to a cooling rack and cool for 3 minutes.
7. When slightly cooled, place the eggplant on a cutting board and slice each slab crosswise into ½-inch strips.
8. Add the eggplant to the serving bowl with the onion mixture. Gently toss everything together, and serve warm or at room temperature.

PER SERVING

Calories: 159 Fat: 4g Carbs: 26g Protein: 6g

Mediterranean Lentils and Rice
Prep time: 5 minutes| Cook time: 25 minutes| Serves 4

- 2¼ cups low-sodium or no-salt-added vegetable broth
- ½ cup uncooked brown or green lentils
- ½ cup uncooked instant brown rice
- ½ cup diced carrots (about 1 carrot)
- ½ cup diced celery (about 1 stalk)
- 1 (2.25-ounce) can sliced olives, drained (about ½ cup)
- ¼ cup diced red onion (about 1/8 onion)
- ¼ cup chopped fresh curly-leaf parsley
- 1½ tablespoons extra-virgin olive oil
- 1 tablespoon freshly squeezed lemon juice (from about ½ small lemon)
- 1 garlic clove, minced (about ½ teaspoon)
- ¼ teaspoon kosher or sea salt
- ¼ teaspoon freshly ground black pepper

1. In a medium saucepan over high heat, bring the broth and lentils to a boil, cover, and lower the heat to medium-low. Cook for 8 minutes.
2. Raise the heat to medium, and stir in the rice. Cover the pot and cook the mixture for 15 minutes, or until the liquid is absorbed. Remove the pot from the heat and let it sit, covered, for 1 minute, then stir.
3. While the lentils and rice are cooking, mix together the carrots, celery, olives, onion, and parsley in a large serving bowl.
4. In a small bowl, whisk together the oil, lemon juice, garlic, salt, and pepper. Set aside. When the lentils and rice are cooked, add them to the serving bowl.
5. Pour the dressing on top, and mix everything together. Serve warm or cold, or store in a sealed container in the refrigerator for up to 7 days.

PER SERVING

Calories: 230 Fat: 8g Carbs: 34g Protein: 8g.

Brown Rice Pilaf with Golden Raisins
Prep time: 5 minutes| Cook time: 15 minutes| Serves 6

- 1 tablespoon extra-virgin olive oil
- 1 cup chopped onion (about ½ medium onion)
- ½ cup shredded carrot (about 1 medium carrot)
- 1 teaspoon ground cumin
- ½ teaspoon ground cinnamon

- 2 cups instant brown rice
- 1¾ cups 100% orange juice
- ¼ cup water
- 1 cup golden raisins
- ½ cup shelled pistachios
- Chopped fresh chives (optional)

1. In a medium saucepan over medium-high heat, heat the oil. Add the onion and cook for 5 minutes, stirring frequently.
2. Add the carrot, cumin, and cinnamon, and cook for 1 minute, stirring frequently. Stir in the rice, orange juice, and water.
3. Bring to a boil, cover, then lower the heat to medium-low. Simmer for 7 minutes, or until the rice is cooked through and the liquid is absorbed. Stir in the raisins, pistachios, and chives (if using) and serve.

PER SERVING

Calories: 320 Fat: 7g Carbs: 61g Protein: 6g

Quinoa and Chickpea Vegetable Bowls
Prep time: 15 minutes| Cook time: 15 minutes| Serves 4

- 1 cup red dry quinoa, rinsed and drained
- 2 cups low-sodium vegetable soup
- 2 cups fresh spinach
- 2 cups finely shredded red cabbage
- 1 (15-ounce / 425-g) can chickpeas, drained and rinsed
- 1 ripe avocado, thinly sliced
- 1 cup shredded carrots
- 1 red bell pepper, thinly sliced
- 4 tablespoons Mango Sauce
- ½ cup fresh cilantro, chopped
- Mango Sauce:
- 1 mango, diced
- ¼ cup fresh lime juice
- ½ teaspoon ground turmeric
- 1 teaspoon finely minced fresh ginger
- ¼ teaspoon sea salt
- Pinch of ground red pepper
- 1 teaspoon pure maple syrup
- 2 tablespoons extra-virgin olive oil

1. Pour the quinoa and vegetable soup in a saucepan. Bring to a boil. Reduce the heat to low. Cover and cook for 15 minutes or until tender. Fluffy with a fork.
2. Meanwhile, combine the ingredients for the mango sauce in a food processor. Pulse until smooth.
3. Divide the quinoa, spinach, and cabbage into 4 serving bowls, then top with chickpeas, avocado, carrots, and bell pepper.
4. Dress them with the mango sauce and spread with cilantro. Serve immediately.

PER SERVING

Calories: 366 Fat: 11.1g Protein: 15.5g Carbs: 55.6g..

Ritzy Veggie Chili

Prep time: 15 minutes| Cook time: 5 hours| Serves 4

- 1 (28-ounce / 794-g) can chopped tomatoes, with the juice
- 1 (15-ounce / 425-g) can black beans, drained and rinsed
- 1 (15-ounce / 425-g) can redly beans, drained and rinsed
- 1 medium green bell pepper, chopped
- 1 yellow onion, chopped
- 1 tablespoon onion powder
- 1 teaspoon paprika
- 1 teaspoon cayenne pepper
- 1 teaspoon garlic powder
- ½ teaspoon sea salt
- ½ teaspoon ground black pepper
- 1 tablespoon olive oil
- 1 large Hass avocado, pitted, peeled, and chopped, for garnish

1. Combine all the ingredients, except for the avocado, in the slow cooker. Stir to mix well.
2. Put the slow cooker lid on and cook on high for 5 hours or until the vegetables are tender and the mixture has a thick consistency.
3. Pour the chili in a large serving bowl. Allow to cool for 30 minutes, then spread with chopped avocado and serve.

PER SERVING

Calories: 633 Fat: 16.3g Protein: 31.7g Carbs: 97.0g..

Spicy Italian Bean Balls with Marinara

Prep time: 15 minutes| Cook time: 45 minutes| Serves 2-4

Bean Balls:
- 1 tablespoon extra-virgin olive oil
- ½ yellow onion, minced
- 1 teaspoon fennel seeds
- 2 teaspoons dried oregano
- ½ teaspoon crushed red pepper flakes
- 1 teaspoon garlic powder
- 1 (15-ounce / 425-g) can white beans (cannellini or navy), drained and rinsed
- ½ cup whole-grain bread crumbs
- Sea salt and ground black pepper, to taste
- Marinara:
- 1 tablespoon extra-virgin olive oil
- 3 garlic cloves, minced
- Handful basil leaves
- 1 (28-ounce / 794-g) can chopped tomatoes with juice reserved
- Sea salt, to taste

1. Preheat the oven to 350°F (180°C). Line a baking sheet with parchment paper. Heat the olive oil in a nonstick skillet over medium heat until shimmering.
2. Add the onion and sauté for 5 minutes or until translucent. Sprinkle with fennel seeds, oregano, red pepper flakes, and garlic powder, then cook for 1 minute or until aromatic.
3. Pour the sautéed mixture in a food processor and add the beans and bread crumbs. Sprinkle with salt and ground black pepper, then pulse to combine well and the mixture holds together.
4. Shape the mixture into balls with a 2-ounce (57-g) cookie scoop, then arrange the balls on the baking sheet.
5. Bake in the preheated oven for 30 minutes or until lightly browned. Flip the balls halfway through the cooking time.
6. While baking the bean balls, heat the olive oil in a saucepan over medium-high heat until shimmering. Add the garlic and basil and sauté for 2 minutes or until fragrant.
7. Fold in the tomatoes and juice. Bring to a boil. Reduce the heat to low. Put the lid on and simmer for 15 minutes. Sprinkle with salt.
8. Transfer the bean balls on a large plate and baste with marinara before serving.

PER SERVING

Calories: 351 Fat: 16.4g Protein: 11.5g Carbs: 42.9g

Fried Cauliflower Rice

Prep time: 5 minutes | Cook time: 20 minutes | Serves 4

- 2 tbsp. of neutral oil (like coconut, vegetable, or peanut)
- 1 head of cauliflower, cut in florets
- 1 bunch of scallions, thinly sliced
- 1 tbsp. of minced fresh ginger
- 3 cloves of garlic, minced
- 2 peeled carrots, diced
- 1 diced red bell pepper
- 2 diced celery stalks
- 1 cup of frozen peas
- 3 tbsp. of soy sauce
- 2 tbsp. of rice vinegar
- 2 tsp. of Sriracha, or some more to taste
- Garnishes:
- 4 eggs
- 1 tbsp. of neutral oil (like coconut, vegetable, or peanut)
- Salt & black pepper, freshly ground
- 4 tbsp. of scallions, thinly sliced
- 4 tbsp. of chopped cilantro (fresh)
- 4 tbsp. of sesame seeds

1. In a bowl of a food processor, pulse cauliflower for two to three minutes, or till the mixture resembles rice. Place aside.
2. Over medium heat, warm the oil in a large skillet. Stir-fry the scallions, ginger, and garlic for approximately a minute or until aromatic.
3. Stir-fry the celery, carrots, and red bell pepper after adding them for 9 to 11 minutes, or until the veggies are soft.
4. Add cauliflower rice & stir-fry for an additional 3 to 5 minutes, or until it starts to turn golden. The frozen peas are added, and they are well mixed up.
5. Stir in the soy sauce, Sriracha, and rice vinegar after adding them. Place aside.
6. Heat the oil into a medium pan over medium to high heat. Directly into the pan, crack the eggs, and cook for 3 to 4 minutes, or till the whites are set the yolks yet are still runny. Add salt and pepper to each.

7. Four plates with cauliflower rice and fried eggs should be used for serving. Add one tsp. of sesame seeds, one tbsp. of cilantro, and one tbsp. of scallions to each dish. Serve right away.

PER SERVING

Total Calories: 291kcal, Fats: 7g, Carbohydrates: 23g, Protein: 13g, Fiber: 4g, Sodium: 100mg, Potassium: 95mg ..

Baked Rolled Oat with Pears and Pecans

Prep time: 15 minutes | Cook time: 30 minutes | Serves 6

- 2 tablespoons coconut oil, melted, plus more for greasing the pan
- 3 ripe pears, cored and diced
- 2 cups unsweetened almond milk
- 1 tablespoon pure vanilla extract
- ¼ cup pure maple syrup
- 2 cups gluten-free rolled oats
- ½ cup raisins
- ¾ cup chopped pecans
- ¼ teaspoon ground nutmeg
- 1 teaspoon ground cinnamon
- ½ teaspoon ground ginger
- ¼ teaspoon sea salt

1. Preheat the oven to 350°f (180°c). Grease a baking dish with melted coconut oil, then spread the pears in a single layer on the baking dish evenly.
2. Combine the almond milk, vanilla extract, maple syrup, and coconut oil in a bowl. Stir to mix well.
3. Combine the remaining ingredients in a separate large bowl. Stir to mix well. Fold the almond milk mixture in the bowl, then pour the mixture over the pears.
4. Place the baking dish in the preheated oven and bake for 30 minutes or until lightly browned and set. Serve immediately.

PER SERVING

Calories: 479 Fat: 34.9g Protein: 8.8g Carbs: 50.1g..

Brown Rice Pilaf with Pistachios and Raisins

Prep time: 15 minutes| Cook time: 15 minutes| Serves 6

- 1 tablespoon extra-virgin olive oil
- 1 cup chopped onion
- ½ cup shredded carrot
- ½ teaspoon ground cinnamon
- 1 teaspoon ground cumin
- 2 cups brown rice
- 1¾ cups pure orange juice
- ¼ cup water
- ½ cup shelled pistachios
- 1 cup golden raisins
- ½ cup chopped fresh chives

1. Heat the olive oil in a saucepan over medium-high heat until shimmering. Add the onion and sauté for 5 minutes or until translucent.
2. Add the carrots, cinnamon, and cumin, then sauté for 1 minutes or until aromatic.
3. Pour int the brown rice, orange juice, and water. Bring to a boil. Reduce the heat to medium-low and simmer for 7 minutes or until the liquid is almost absorbed.
4. Transfer the rice mixture in a large serving bowl, then spread with pistachios, raisins, and chives. Serve immediately.

PER SERVING

Calories: 264 Fat: 7.1g Protein: 5.2g Carbs: 48.9g.

Red Lentils Curry

Prep time: 15 minutes | Cook time: 30 minutes | Serves 6

- 1/2 onion (large), diced
- 1 1/2 cups of lentils, rinsed & picked over
- 2 tbsp. of butter
- 1/2 tbsp. of garam masala
- 2 tbsp. of red curry paste
- 1 tsp. of curry powder
- 1 tsp. of sugar
- 1/2 tsp. of turmeric
- 1 tsp. of garlic, minced
- Some sprinkles of cayenne pepper
- 1 tsp. of minced ginger
- 1 can of tomato puree (14-ounce)
- Some cilantro to garnish
- 1/4 cup of coconut cream or milk
- Some rice to serve

1. The lentils should be prepared as directed. Drain then set apart.
2. In a big pan over medium-high heat, melt the butter. When aromatic and golden, add onion and continue to cook for a few minutes. Stir-fry for 1-2 minutes after adding all the spices (garam masala, curry paste, curry powder, cayenne, turmeric, garlic, sugar, and ginger). When smooth, whisk in the tomato puree and continue to boil.
3. Add the cream & lentils. Simmer for a further 15

to 20 minutes (the more, the better) and stir to blend! Garnish with cilantro & serve with rice.

PER SERVING

Total Calories: 249kcal, Fats: 6.5g, Carbohydrates: 35.1g, Protein: 12.5g, Fiber: 14.5g, Sodium: 181.9mg, Potassium: 650.3mg ..

Sweet Potatoes with White Beans and Lemony Kale

Prep time: 15 minutes | Cook time: 55 minutes | Serves 4

- 1 tbsp. of olive oil, optional
- 4 large/ medium sweet potatoes
- 1 chopped shallot or any other onion
- 1 tsp. of lemon zest
- 1 - 2 cloves of garlic, minced
- ½ to 1 tsp. of sea salt, to taste
- 1 can of cannellini beans, 15 oz. (about almost 2 cups of cooked beans)
- 1 bunch of kale (chopped), remove thick stems (can substitute baby kale, collards, spinach, chard, etc.)
- ½ to 1 tsp. of red pepper flakes (crushed), optional
- Some tamari pumpkin seeds, toasted
- juice from 1/2 a lemon

1. Turn the oven on to 350 degrees. Dry and wash the sweet potatoes. With a fork, prick the tops many times. Place onto a baking sheet, and depending on size, bake for 45 to 60 minutes, or until tender.
2. A sauté pan should be heated to medium. Including oil, add it now. Stirring sporadically throughout the next two minutes, add the shallot. Cook for one minute after adding the salt, garlic, and lemon zest. When the kale is reduced and attains a deep green color, add the beans and red pepper flakes, and continue to simmer, stirring periodically, for another 2 to 3 minutes, including the lemon juice Season to taste and make any adjustments. Get rid of the heat.
3. Let the sweet potatoes cool a little. Add the kale & bean combination, followed by the pumpkin seeds, to each. Or, if you're preparing food, let everything cool. For up to 3-4 days, keep the potato and bean combination separate in the fridge.

PER SEVING

Total Calories: 295kcal, Fats: 8.5g, Carbohydrates: 46g, Protein: 12g, Fiber: 11g, Sodium: 529mg, Potassium: 150mg

Cherry, Apricot, and Pecan Brown Rice Bowl

Prep time: 15 minutes | Cook time: 1 hour & 5 minutes | Serves 2

- 2 tablespoons olive oil
- 2 green onions, sliced
- ½ cup brown rice
- 1 cup low -sodium chicken stock
- 2 tablespoons dried cherries
- 4 dried apricots, chopped
- 2 tablespoons pecans, toasted and chopped
- Sea salt and freshly ground pepper, to taste

1. Heat the olive oil in a medium saucepan over medium-high heat until shimmering. Add the green onions and sauté for 1 minutes or until fragrant.
2. Add the rice. Stir to mix well, then pour in the chicken stock. Bring to a boil. Reduce the heat to low. Cover and simmer for 50 minutes or until the brown rice is soft.
3. Add the cherries, apricots, and pecans, and simmer for 10 more minutes or until the fruits are tender.
4. Pour them in a large serving bowl. Fluff with a fork. Sprinkle with sea salt and freshly ground pepper. Serve immediately.

PER SERVING

Calories: 451 Fat: 25.9g Protein: 8.2g Carbs: 50.4g ..

Mediterranean Cauliflower Rice

Prep time: 10 minutes | Cook time: 10 minutes | Serves 4

- 1 tbsp. of olive oil
- 1 head of cauliflower (medium), about 3 cups
- 1/4 cup of onion, chopped
- 1 tbsp. of lemon juice
- 2 cloves of garlic, minced
- zest from 1/2 a lemon
- 1/4 tsp. of red chili flakes
- 2 tbsp. of pine nuts
- chopped fresh parsley

1. Prepare the cauliflower by removing the leaves and stalks and chopping it into florets of various sizes. Cauliflower florets should be pushed into a food processor that is running with a grating attachment.
2. Alternately, use a box grater to rice the cauliflower.
3. In a big skillet, heat the olive oil. The onion should be added to the heated oil and cooked for 4 to 5 minutes on medium heat or until tender and transparent. For one more minute, add the garlic.
4. Cauliflower should be added to the skillet. To thoroughly combine everything, stir.
5. Then add the pine nuts, chile flakes, lemon zest, and high heat. One more minute of cooking. The cauliflower won't get too mushy because of the high heat's ability to remove extra moisture.
6. Add the parsley after turning the heat off. Serve warm and take a sip after tasting; add additional salt if necessary.

PER SERVING

Total Calories: 71kcal, Fats: 2g, Carbohydrates: 8g, Protein: 3g, Fiber: 2g, Sodium: 38mg, Potassium: 50mg

Chipotle, Pinto, and Black Bean and Corn Succotash

Prep time: 5 minutes| Cook time: 10 minutes| Serves 2

- 2 tablespoons extra-virgin olive oil
- 1 1/2 cups fresh or frozen corn
- 1 cup black beans, chopped
- 2 green onions, white and green parts, sliced
- 1/2 tablespoon minced garlic
- 1 medium tomato, chopped
- 1 teaspoon chili powder
- 1/2 teaspoon chipotle powder
- 1/2 teaspoon ground cumin
- 1 (14-ounce) can pinto beans, drained and rinsed
- 1 teaspoon sea salt, or to taste

1. Heat the olive oil in a large skillet over medium heat. Add the corn, black beans, green onions, and garlic and stir for 5 minutes.
2. Add the tomato, chili powder, chipotle powder, and cumin and stir for 3 minutes, until the tomato starts to soften.
3. In a bowl, mash some of the pinto beans with a fork. Add all of the beans to the skillet and stir for 2 minutes, until the beans are heated through.
4. Remove from the heat and stir in the salt. Serve hot or warm.

PER SERVING

Calories: 391Fat: 16gCarbs: 53g Fiber: 15gSugar: 4g Protein: 15g Sodium: 253mg

Mixed Vegetable Medley

Prep time: 5 minutes| Cook time: 20 minutes| Serves 2

- 1 stick (1/2 cup) unsalted butter, divided
- 1 large potato, cut into 1/2-inch dice
- 1 onion, chopped
- 1/2 tablespoon minced garlic
- 1 cup pinto beans, chopped
- 2 ears fresh sweet corn, kernels removed
- 1 red bell pepper, seeded and cut into strips
- 2 cups sliced white mushrooms
- Salt
- Freshly ground black pepper

1. Heat half of the butter in a large nonstick skillet over medium-high heat. When the butter is frothy, add the potato and cook, stirring frequently, for 15 minutes, until golden.
2. Turn the heat down slightly if the butter begins to burn.
3. Add the remaining butter, turn down the heat to medium, and add the onion, garlic, pinto beans, and corn. Cook, stirring frequently, for 5 minutes.
4. Add the red bell pepper and mushrooms. Stir for another 5 minutes, until the vegetables are tender and the mushrooms have browned but are still plump. Add more butter, if necessary.
5. Remove from heat and season with salt and pepper. Serve hot.

PER SERVING

Calories: 688 Fat: 48g Carbs: 63g Fiber: 11g Sugar: 11g Protein: 11g Sodium: 360mg

Spicy Lentils with Spinach

Prep time: 5 minutes| Cook time: 25 minutes| Serves 4

- 1 cup dried red lentils, well-rinsed
- 2 1/2 cups water
- 1 tablespoon extra-virgin olive oil
- 1 tablespoon minced garlic
- 1 teaspoon ground cumin
- 1/2 teaspoon ground coriander
- 1/2 teaspoon turmeric
- 1/4 teaspoon cayenne pepper
- 1 medium tomato, chopped
- 1 (16-ounce) package spinach
- 1 teaspoon salt
- Freshly ground black pepper

1. In a medium saucepan, bring the lentils and water to a boil.
2. Partially cover the pot, reduce the heat to medium, and simmer, stirring occasionally, until the lentils are tender, about 15 minutes.
3. Drain the lentils and set aside.
4. In a large nonstick skillet, heat the olive oil over medium heat. When hot, add the garlic, cumin, coriander, turmeric, and cayenne. Sauté for 2 minutes.
5. Stir in the tomato and cook for another 3 to 5 minutes, until the tomato begins to break apart and the mixture thickens somewhat.
6. Add handfuls of the spinach at a time, stirring until wilted.
7. Stir in the drained lentils and cook for another few minutes.
8. Season with salt and freshly ground black pepper and serve hot.

PER SERVING

Calories: 237 Fat: 5g Carbs: 35g Fiber: 18g Sugar: 2g Protein: 16g Sodium: 677mg

Pinto and Black Bean Fry with Couscous

Prep time: 5 minutes| Cook time: 20 minutes| Serves 4

- 1/2 cup water
- 1/3 cup couscous (semolina or whole-wheat)
- 2 tablespoons extra-virgin olive oil
- 1 small onion, chopped
- 1/2 tablespoon minced garlic
- 1 cup black beans, cut into 1-inch pieces
- 1 cup fresh or frozen corn
- 11/2 teaspoons chili powder
- 1/2 teaspoon ground cumin
- 1 large tomato, finely chopped
- 1 (14-ounce) can pinto beans, drained and rinsed
- 1 teaspoon salt

1. Bring the water to a boil in a small saucepan. Remove from the heat and stir in the couscous. Cover the pan and let sit for 10 minutes.
2. Gently fluff the couscous with a fork.
3. While the couscous is cooking, heat the olive oil in a large skillet over medium heat. Add the onion and garlic and stir for 1 minute.
4. Add the black beans and stir for 4 minutes, until they begin to soften.
5. Add the corn, stir for another 2 minutes, then add the chili powder and cumin, and stir to coat the vegetables.
6. Add the tomato and simmer for 3 or 4 minutes. Stir in the pinto beans and couscous and cook for 3 to 4 minutes, until everything is heated throughout. Stir often.
7. Stir in the salt and serve hot or warm.

PER SERVING

Calories: 267 Fat: 8g Carbs: 41g Fiber: 10g Sugar: 4g Protein: 10g Sodium: 601mg

Indonesian-Style Spicy Fried Tempeh Strips

Prep time: 5 minutes| Cook time: 20 minutes| Serves 4

- 1 cup sesame oil, or as needed
- 1 (12-ounce) package tempeh, cut into narrow 2-inch strips
- 2 medium onions, sliced
- 11/2 tablespoons tomato paste
- 3 teaspoons tamari or soy sauce
- 1 teaspoon dried red chili flakes
- 1/2 teaspoon brown sugar
- 2 tablespoons lime juice

1. Heat the sesame oil in a large wok or saucepan over medium-high heat. Add more sesame oil as needed to raise the level to at least 1 inch.
2. As soon as the oil is hot but not smoking, add the tempeh slices and cook, stirring frequently, for 10 minutes, until a light golden color on all sides.
3. Add the onions and stir for another 10 minutes,

until the tempeh and onions are brown and crispy.
4. Remove with a slotted spoon and add to a large bowl lined with several sheets of paper towel.
5. While the tempeh and onions are cooking, whisk together the tomato paste, tamari or soy sauce, red chili flakes, brown sugar, and lime juice in a small bowl.
6. Remove the paper towel from the large bowl and pour the sauce over the tempeh strips. Mix well to coat.

PER SERVING

Calories: 317 Fat: 23g Carbs: 15g Sugar: 4g Protein: 17g Sodium: 266mg

Vegetable Rice

Prep time: 5 minutes| Cook time: 25 minutes| Serves 4

- 3/4 cup uncooked short- or long-grain white rice
- 1 1/2 cups water
- 2 tablespoons sesame oil, divided
- 2 carrots, diced
- 1 tablespoon minced garlic
- 6 green onions, white and green parts, sliced and divided
- 2 tablespoons tamari or soy sauce
- 1/2 cup frozen green peas, defrosted

1. Rinse the rice and add to a small saucepan. Add the water and bring to a boil.
2. Reduce the heat to low, cover, and simmer for 15 minutes, until the water is absorbed. Fluff with a fork and set aside.
3. While the rice is cooking, heat 1/2 tablespoon of the sesame oil in a large saucepan or wok over medium heat.
4. Cook without stirring for 5 minutes. Remove to a plate and cut into small strips. Set aside.
5. Return the saucepan or wok to the heat. Heat the remaining 2 1/2 tablespoons of sesame oil. Add the carrots and stir for 2 minutes.
6. Add the mushrooms, garlic, and the white parts of the green onions. Stir for 3 more minutes.
7. Add the cooked rice and tamari or soy sauce. Cook, stirring frequently, for 10 minutes, until the rice is sticky.
8. Toss in the green parts of the green onions, and peas and stir to mix. Remove from the heat and serve hot with extra tamari or soy sauce, if desired.

PER SERVING

Calories: 271 Fat: 10g Carbs: 37g Fiber: 3g Sugar: 4g Protein: 9g Sodium: 567mg

Spanish-Style Saffron Rice with Black Beans

Prep time: 5 minutes| Cook time: 25 minutes| Serves 4

- 2 cups vegetable stock
- 1/4 teaspoon saffron threads (optional)
- 1 1/2 tablespoons extra-virgin olive oil
- 1 small red or yellow onion, halved and thinly sliced
- 1 tablespoon minced garlic
- 1 teaspoon turmeric
- 2 teaspoons paprika
- 1 cup long-grain white rice, well-rinsed
- 1 (14-ounce) can black beans, drained and rinsed
- 1/2 cup pinto beans, halved or quartered
- 1 small red bell pepper, chopped
- 1 teaspoon salt

1. In a small pot, heat the vegetable stock until boiling. Add the saffron, if using, and remove from the heat.
2. Meanwhile, heat the olive oil in a large nonstick skillet over medium heat.
3. Add the onion, garlic, turmeric, paprika, and rice and stir to coat.
4. Pour in the stock, and mix in the black beans, pinto beans, and red bell pepper.
5. Bring to a boil, reduce the heat to medium-low, cover, and simmer until the rice is tender and most of the liquid has been absorbed, about 20 minutes.
6. Stir in the salt and serve hot.

PER SERVING

Calories: 332 Fat: 5g Carbs: 63g Fiber: 9g Sugar: 2g Protein: 11g Sodium: 658mg

Simple Lemon Dal

Prep time: 5 minutes| Cook time: 25 minutes| Serves 4

- For the lentils
- 1 cup dried red lentils, well-rinsed
- 2 1/2 cups water
- 1/2 teaspoon turmeric
- 1/2 teaspoon ground cumin
- 2 tablespoons lemon juice
- 1/3cup fresh parsley, chopped
- 1 teaspoon salt
- For finishing
- 1 tablespoon extra-virgin olive oil
- 2 teaspoons minced garlic
- 1/2 teaspoon dried red chili flakes or ¼ teaspoon cayenne pepper

1. Add the lentils to a medium saucepan and pour in the water. Stir in the turmeric and cumin and bring to a boil.
2. Reduce the heat to medium-low, cover, and simmer, stirring occasionally, for 20 minutes, until the lentils are soft and the mixture has thickened.
3. Stir in the lemon juice, parsley, and salt, and re-

move the pan from the heat.
4. In a small saucepan, heat the oil over medium-high heat. When hot, add the garlic and red chili flakes or cayenne, and stir for 1 minute.
5. Quickly pour the oil into the cooked lentils, cover, and let sit for 5 minutes.
6. Stir the lentils and serve immediately.

PER SERVING

Calories: 207 Fat: 4g Carbs: 30g Fiber: 15g Sugar: 1g Protein: 13g Sodium: 589mg

Cauliflower Latke

Prep time: 15 minutes | Cook time: 30 minutes | Serves 4

- 12 oz. cauliflower rice, cooked
- 1 egg, beaten
- 1/3 cup corn starch
- Salt and pepper to taste
- ¼ cup vegetable oil, divided
- Chopped onion chives

1. Squeeze excess water from the cauliflower rice using paper towels.
2. Place the cauliflower rice in a bowl.
3. Stir in the egg and cornstarch.
4. Season with salt and pepper.
5. Fill 2 tablespoons of oil into a pan over medium heat.
6. Add 2 to 3 tablespoons of the cauliflower mixture into the pan.
7. Cook for 3 minutes each side.
8. Repeat until you've used up the rest of the batter.
9. Garnish with chopped chives.

PER SERVING

Calories:209 ; Fiber:1.9g ;Protein:3.4g

Brussels Sprouts Hash

Prep time: 30 minutes| Cook time: 20 minutes| Serves 4

- 1 lb. Brussels sprouts, sliced in half
- 1 tablespoon olive oil
- Salt and pepper to taste
- 2 teaspoons balsamic vinegar
- ¼ cup goat cheese, crumbled

1. Preheat your oven to 400 degrees F.
2. Coat the Brussels sprouts with oil.
3. Sprinkle with salt and pepper.
4. Transfer to a baking pan.
5. Roast in the oven for 20 minutes.
6. Drizzle with the vinegar.
7. Sprinkle with the seeds and cheese before serving.
8.

PER SERVING

Calories:117; Fiber: 4.8g; Protein: 5.8g

Brussels Sprouts Chips

Prep time: 10 minutes| Cook time: 0 minute| Serves 6

- 3 tablespoons lemon juice
- ¼ cup olive oil
- Salt and pepper to taste
- 1 lb. Brussels sprouts, sliced thinly
- ½ cup pecans, toasted and chopped

1. Mix the lemon juice, olive oil, salt and pepper in a bowl.
2. Toss the Brussels sprouts, and pecans in this mixture.

PER SERVING

Calories:245; Protein: 6.4g;Fiber:5g.

Vegan Potato Pancakes

Prep time: 5 minutes| Cook time: 10 minutes| Serves 10

- ½ yellow onion (grated)
- ¼ teaspoons baking powder
- Salt and pepper to taste
- 3 russet potato (grated)
- ½ cup all-purpose flour
- vegetable oil for frying
- 2 green onion (chopped)

1. In a large bowl, mix everything together.
2. Heat about 1 tablespoon of oil in a frying pan over medium-high heat. Once hot, form a loose patty out of the potato mixture.
3. When the oil is hot, drop the patty directly into the frying pan.
4. After frying the bottom for a few minutes, flip over and fry the other side.
5. Repeat with remaining potato mixture until all of it is consumed. If necessary, add more oil to the pan.

PER SERVING

Calories: 70; Carbs:10g;Protein:2.1g;Fat:1g

Mushroom Burgers

Prep time: 15 minutes | Cook time: 50 minutes | Serves 6

- 1 peeled sweet potato (medium), about 9 ounces, sliced thinly
- 2 tsp. of olive oil, divided
- 16 ounces of mushrooms, cleaned & sliced
- 1/4 cup of walnuts
- 1 red onion (medium), sliced
- 1/4 tsp. of red pepper flakes
- 1/4 tsp. of onion powder
- 1/2 tsp. of Italian seasoning
- 1/4 tsp. of garlic powder
- 1/4 tsp. of sea salt, some more to taste
- 1/2 tsp. of ginger powder
- 1/4 tsp. of black pepper, some more to taste
- 1 egg
- 3/4 cup of almond flour
- 1 tsp. of chia seeds

1. Heat the oven up to 400 °F.
2. Put the sweet potato onto a parchment paper–covered sheet tray. Add 1 teaspoon of sea salt, 1 teaspoon of pepper, and 1 teaspoon of olive oil. To become tender when forked, roast for 15-20 minutes.
3. Cook the mushrooms & onions for approximately 10 minutes over high heat, or until they are tender and the liquid has completely evaporated.
4. Let the mushrooms and sweet potatoes cool until they are not hot to the touch.
5. Add the combination of mushrooms, sweet potatoes, walnuts, herbs, salt, and pepper. Also, include the egg & chia seeds. Don't over-process the mixture; simply pulse a few times to blend. The sweet potato pieces should be the size of peas.
6. Lower the oven's temperature to 350 °F and line a sheet pan with parchment paper.
7. Create six 1-inch patties out of the sweet potato & mushroom mixture.
8. Cook the burgers for a further 5 minutes after flipping them after baking for 30 minutes. Serve warm with your preferred toppings after 5 minutes of cooling.

PER SERVING

Total Calories: 129kcal, Fats: 8.1g, Carbohydrates: 10g, Protein: 6.5g, Fiber: 3.8g, Sodium: 102mg, Potassium: 200mg

Pegan Pancakes

Prep time: 5 minutes | Cook time: 15 minutes | Serves 4

- 3/4 cup of tapioca flour
- 1 cup of almond flour
- 1 tbsp. of baking powder
- 2/3 cup of unsweetened almond milk
- 1/4 tsp. of sea salt
- 2 tsp. of apple cider vinegar
- 1 tbsp. of coconut oil, melted
- 1 tbsp. of maple syrup
- 1 tsp. Of pure vanilla extract

1. In a blender, combine all the ingredients. After a brief period of blending, stop the blender, scrape the sides, and resume blending. However, as mentioned above, mixing does assist in making these pancakes fluffier. The batter may also be made in a bowl.
2. If extra liquid or flour is required, add it gradually (1/2 Tbsp. at a time) to get the desired consistency for pancake batter.
3. Pour roughly a scant 1/4 cup batter for each pancake onto an oiled skillet over medium-high heat.
4. Flip pancakes when they start to bubble or when a spatula can easily slide under one. Cook the food further until both sides are golden brown.
5. Before consuming pancakes, give them a little time to cool.
6. Add the preferred garnishes, such as Strawberry Vanilla Roasted Bean Sauce and nut butter.

PER SERVING

Total Calories: 283kcal, Fats: 18g, Carbohydrates: 29g, Protein: 6g, Fiber: 3g, Sodium: 200mg, Potassium: 15mg

Broccoli with Lemon

Prep time: 15 minutes| Cook time: 15 minutes| Serves 8

- 2 lemons, sliced in half
- 1 lb. broccoli
- 2 tablespoons sesame oil, toasted
- Salt and pepper to taste
- 1 tablespoon sesame seeds, toasted

1. Fill oil into a pan over medium heat.
2. Add the lemons and cook until caramelized.
3. Transfer to a plate.
4. Put the broccoli in the pan and cook for 8 minutes.
5. Squeeze the lemons to release juice in a bowl.
6. Stir in the oil, salt and pepper.
7. Coat the broccoli rabe with the mixture.
8. Sprinkle seeds on top.

PER SERVING

Calories:59; Carbs:4.1g;Protein:2.2g

Vegetable Frittata

Prep time: 10 minutes | Cook time: 50 minutes | Serves 6

- 2 diced potatoes (medium), (without or with the skin)
- 1 tbsp. of olive oil or 1/4 cup of water
- 1 onion (small), diced
- 1 diced zucchini
- 1 diced bell pepper
- 2 cloves of garlic, minced
- A pinch of red pepper flakes (optional)
- A handful of grape tomatoes, quartered or halved
- Some mineral salt & pepper to taste

For the food processor/blender
- 1/4 cup of non-dairy milk, unsweetened
- 1 package of organic silken tofu (16 oz.), firm or soft, drained
- 2 heaping tsp. of corn starch, tapioca, or arrowroot flour
- 1 tsp. of mustard (any) or 1/2 tsp. of mustard powder
- 2 – 3 tbsp. of nutritional yeast
- 1 1/2 tsp. of tarragon, basil, or thyme, dried (or a combo)
- 1/2 tsp. of salt
- 1/2 tsp. of garlic powder
- 1/8 tsp. of pepper (white or black)
- 1/4 tsp. of turmeric

1. Set oven up to 375 degrees Fahrenheit.
2. In a skillet with medium heat, add the oil and the potatoes, and cook for 5 minutes. Then, add the onion and cook for 5 more minutes. When softened, add bell pepper, zucchini, and garlic. Cook for a further minute or two after adding tomatoes and red pepper flakes (optional). To taste, add salt and black pepper to the food.
3. The remaining ingredients should be combined and blended into a smooth tofu egg in a food processor or blender for seasoning and taste.
4. Stir the tofu mixture well into the pan in which the veggies have been cooking. Pour the mixture into a springform pan or a 9-inch round pie/quiche dish that has been gently buttered. Make sure all of the borders are filled before using a spoon or

spatula to level the top flat.

5. Frittata must be solid to the touch after 35 to 45 minutes of baking when placed on the center rack. Cover the top with foil or a tiny Silpat if the browning gets out of hand. Remove and let cool for ten minutes minimum. When using a pie or quiche dish, release the frittata's sides, set a plate on top, and delicately turn it over, so it falls into the plate. Then, serve.

PER SERVING

Total Calories: 139kcal, Fats: 3.5g, Carbohydrates: 17.7g, Protein: 9.5g, Fiber: 3.3g, Sodium: 236.5mg, Potassium: 12mg

---

Sheet Pan Fajitas

Prep time: 15 minutes | Cook time: 25 minutes | Serves 4

- 1 thinly sliced orange bell pepper
- 1 thinly sliced red bell pepper
- 1 thinly sliced green bell pepper
- 1 tbsp. of chili powder
- 2 tbsp. of olive oil
- 1 tbsp. of lime juice, freshly squeezed
- 1 & 1/2 tsp. of ground cumin
- 3 minced cloves of garlic
- 1 tsp. of ground paprika
- Kosher salt & black pepper (freshly ground), to taste
- 1/4 tsp. of onion powder
- 6 eggs (large)
- 1/4 cup of chopped cilantro leaves, fresh
- 1 halved avocado, peeled, seeded & sliced

1. Set oven up to 400 degrees Fahrenheit. Spray nonstick cooking spray or lightly oil the baking sheet.
2. On the prepped baking sheet, spread out the bell peppers into a single layer. Add the garlic, cumin, paprika, onion powder, chili powder, and olive oil, and gently mix to blend. Add salt and pepper to taste.
3. Place in oven and bake for 12 to 15 minutes or until cooked.
4. After removing from the oven, make 6 wells. Add eggs, carefully breaking them all the way through while leaving the yolk undamaged. To taste, add salt and pepper.
5. Place in the oven and bake for a further 8 to 12 minutes, or till the egg whites are set.
6. If preferred, top with avocado & cilantro before serving.

PER SERVING

Total Calories: 261kcal, Fats: 19g, Carbohydrates: 9g, Protein: 12g, Fiber: 3g, Sodium: 378mg, Potassium: 200mg

Zucchini Noodles in Alfredo Sauce

Prep time: 15 minutes | Cook time: 5 minutes | Serves 2

·
- 1-2 tbsp. of Parmesan (optional)
- 2 zucchinis spiralized (medium)
- Alfredo Sauce:
- 2 tbsp. of lemon juice
- ½ cup of cashews (raw), soaked for some hours or in the boiling water for 8-10 minutes
- 3 tbsp. of nutritional yeast
- 1 tsp. of onion powder
- 2 tsp. of white miso (can substitute soy sauce, tamari, or coconut aminos)
- ¼-1/2 cup of water
- ½ tsp. of garlic powder

1. Slice zucchini into noodles, then pat them dry.
2. Starting with 1/4 cup of water, combine all the Alfredo ingredients in a high-speed blender and process until smooth. If the sauce is very thick, add a tablespoon of water at a time till you reach the desired consistency.
3. The zucchini may either be left raw or heated for two to three minutes in a skillet with some olive oil. Note: Avoid overcooking the zoodles as they will get mushy.
4. Alfredo sauce and optional vegan parmesan are served on top of zucchini noodles.

PER SERVING

Total Calories: 225kcal, Fats: 16g, Carbohydrates: 19g, Protein: 14g, Fiber: 6g, Sodium: 200mg, Potassium: 350mg

Shepherd's Vegan Pie

Prep time: 15 minutes | Cook time: 45 minutes | Serves 6

Mashed potatoes:
- 3-4 tbsp. of vegan butter
- 3 pounds of Yukon gold potatoes, thoroughly washed & partially peeled
- Sea salt & black pepper (to taste)
- Filling:
- 1 onion, medium (diced)
- 1 tbsp. of olive oil
- 2 cloves of garlic (minced)
- 1 pinch of sea salt & black pepper each
- 2 tbsp. of tomato paste (optional)
- 1 1/2 cups of uncooked green or brown lentils (rinsed & drained)
- 2 tsp. of thyme, fresh (or substitute 1 tsp. of dried thyme per two tsp., fresh)
- 4 cups of vegetable stock
- 1 bag of mixed veggies, frozen (10-ounce): peas, green beans, carrots, and corn

1. Any large potatoes should be cut in half, put in a big saucepan, and just filled with water. Add salt liberally, bring to a boil over medium-high heat, cover, and simmer for 20 to 30 minutes, or until they easily come off a knife.

2. When done, drain, add to the pot again to help evaporate any water left, and then transfer them to a mixing bowl. Mash the ingredients until smooth using a fork, pastry cutter, or masher. Add the required quantity of vegan butter (original recipe calls for 3-4 Tbsp.; adjust if the batch size is changed), then season with salt & pepper to taste. Set aside and loosely cover.
3. Pre-heat the oven up to 425 degrees F (218 degrees C) while the potatoes are cooking, and gently butter a baking dish (2-quart) (or a dish of a similar size, such as a 9-by-13-inch pan). Adjust the number of dishes used or the size of the dish if the batch size is changed; an 8 by 8 won't quite fit it all.
4. It takes around 5 minutes to softly brown and caramelize the garlic and onions in olive oil in a big pot on medium heat.
5. Add a dash of each salt and pepper, along with the optional tomato paste. Then whisk in the stock, lentils, and thyme. Achieve a low boil. After that, put a lid on it and simmer it. Continue to boil the lentils until they are soft (35-40 minutes). When the food is cooked, take off the top and boil it uncovered for another few minutes, stirring periodically to cook out any extra liquid.
6. Add the frozen vegetables, stir, and cover for the last 10-12 minutes of simmering to combine the flavors.
7. If necessary, taste and adjust the spices. After that, move to the oven-safe baking dish you've prepared and gently add the mashed potatoes on top. With a fork or spoon, smooth down the surface and season with more sea salt and pepper.
8. Place the mashers onto a baking sheet to collect spillover and bake for 10 to 15 minutes, or until the tops are just starting to brown.
9. Let cool momentarily before serving. It will thicken more the longer it sits. Before covering and storing in the refrigerator for up to some days, let it cool fully.

PER SERVING

Total Calories: 396kcal, Fats: 5.3g, Carbohydrates: 72g, Protein: 17.7g, Fiber: 19g, Sodium: 109mg, Potassium: 50mg

Tempeh Lettuce Wraps & Peanut Sauce

Prep time: 20 minutes | Cook time: 10 minutes | Serves 2

- 1 cup of vegetable broth
- 8-ounce tempeh block
- 1 tsp. of soy sauce
- 1/4 tsp. of ground coriander
- 1 tsp. of maple syrup
- 1/8 tsp. of garlic powder
- 1 carrot, (medium) peeled & julienned
- 8 leaves of butter lettuce
- 1 red bell pepper (medium), sliced
- 1 to 1 1/4 cups of red cabbage, thinly sliced
- Some peanut sauce
- Garnish: (optional)
- red pepper flakes
- 1 stalk of sliced scallions

1. Transfer the tempeh cubes to the food processor after cutting them into 1/2-inch pieces. For approximately 5 seconds, blend the tempeh until it is broken up into very little bits. You will notice the smell of fermented soybeans when you open the food processor's cover, and that is quite normal.
2. Vegetable broth, maple syrup, soy sauce, garlic powder, & powdered coriander should all be combined in a bowl.
3. A nonstick sauté pan or skillet should be heated to medium. Add the broth mixture and the tempeh. Cook the tempeh for about 8-9 minutes, stirring regularly, or until the liquids are entirely absorbed. Although the tempeh may seem to be ready to be taken off the heat in 5 minutes, resist the desire to do so. The tempeh isn't yet ready if, while tapping it with the back side of a spatula, you hear a sound like that of walking through rain puddles. You're probably off by a few minutes. Take the pan off the heat when the liquid is absorbed.
4. Put the lettuce wrappers together. Include part of the tempeh as well as the carrots, red bell pepper, cabbage, and lettuce leaves. If desired, top

the filling with peanut sauce and garnish with red pepper flakes and sliced scallions. Serve right away.

PER SERVING

Total Calories: 201kcal, Fats: 7.2g, Carbohydrates: 23.6g, Protein: 14.1g, Fiber: 8.3g, Sodium: 539mg, Potassium: 250mg

Vegetable Ratatouille

Prep time: 10 minutes | Cook time: 25 minutes | Serves 4

- 1 onion (large), diced
- 2 tbsp. of olive oil
- 1 tsp. of red pepper flakes
- 3 (any color) bell peppers
- 1 eggplant (large), about 2 & 1/2 lbs.
- 2 (about 1 lb.) zucchini
- 8 oz. of mushrooms
- 1 (about 1/2 lb.) yellow squash
- 1 tbsp. of garlic, minced
- 2 cans of diced tomatoes (no-salt-added)
- 1 tbsp. of tomato paste
- 2 tbsp. of fresh thyme
- 1/4 cup of fresh parsley
- 1/4 cup of fresh basil
- salt & pepper, to taste
- 1/2 tbsp. of balsamic vinegar
-

1. While preparing the other ingredients, toss the diced eggplant with 1 tbsp. Salt and put aside in a colander. Any bitter fluids will be drawn out by this.
2. Peppers may be roasted until the skin is browned over a gas burner or under a broiler. Remove the peel and seeds after 10 minutes of letting the fruit rest in a plastic bag. Dice.
3. In the meanwhile, warm 2 tablespoons of olive oil into a Dutch oven. In approximately 5 minutes, add the onion & red pepper & cook until barely transparent. Add the salt-free eggplant to the saucepan after giving it a good washing. For approximately 5 minutes, sauté the eggplant, often turning, until it is halfway cooked.
4. Include mushrooms, zucchini, and squash. Add salt & pepper to taste and simmer the mushrooms for 10 minutes or until they start to juice.
5. Add tomato paste & garlic, and simmer for an additional one to two minutes, or until aromatic. 5 more minutes of simmering after adding tomatoes and stirring in roasted peppers.
6. Adjust salt and stir in some fresh herbs, saving some for garnish. Serve either hot or at normal temperature after adding a dash of vinegar to brighten.

PER SERVING

Total Calories: 175kcal, Fats: 5.5g, Carbohydrates: 27.3g, Protein: 6.7g, Fiber: 7.8g, Sodium: 71mg, Potassium: 198mg

Vegan Green Spaghetti

Prep time: 2 to 3 hours| Cook time: 15 to 20 minutes| Serves 8

- 4 roasted poblano chiles, chopped
- 2 chopped garlic cloves
- 1 cup of almond milk, unsweetened
- 2 tablespoon of olive oil
- 1 cup of soaked cashews
- 3 tablespoon of lemon juice
- Half chopped white onion
- Black Pepper, to taste
- 3 tablespoon of cilantro
- ¾ teaspoon of salt
- Pasta
- Half cup of water
- 26 oz. spaghetti

1. Soak the cashews in boiling water for 2 to 3 hours.
2. Sauté onion in hot oil for 3 to 4 minutes, add garlic and cook for 1 to 2 minutes.
3. Add rest of the ingredients and blend with a stick blender, taste and adjust seasoning.
4. Cook pasta as per the pack's instructions, drain all bit half cup of water.
5. Add sauce to the pasta, toss well and serve.

PER SERVING

Calories: 496 Total fat: 13 g Total carbs: 79 g Fiber: 0 g Sugar: 5.3 g Protein: 16 g Sodium: 269 mg

Cucumber and Tomato Gazpacho

Prep time: 10 minutes | Cook time:0 minutes | Serves 4

- 8 ripe plum/heirloom tomatoes
- 1 medium red bell pepper, seeded and coarsely chopped
- 1 medium cucumber, coarsely chopped
- ½ cup extra virgin olive oil
- 1 tablespoon balsamic/red wine vinegar
- salt and pepper as needed
- sunflower seeds for garnish

1. Take your food processor and add tomatoes, pepper, cucumber, and pulse until everything breaks down.
2. While the motor is still running, add oil, and process for about 2 minutes until the mix is smooth and velvety.
3. Add vinegar and process for a few seconds more.
4. Refrigerate the soup for about 2 hours, serve cold with a bit of salt and pepper.
5. Garnish with some seeds if desired.
6. Enjoy!

PER SERVING

Calories: 376 Fat: 34 g Saturated Fat: 5 g Carbohydrates: 20 g Fiber: 2 g Sodium: 258 mg Protein: 4 g

The Healthy Guacamole

Prep time: 10 minutes | Cook time:0 minutes | Serves 3

- 3 large ripe avocados
- 1 large red onion, peeled and diced
- 4 tablespoon of freshly squeezed lime juice
- Salt as needed
- Freshly ground black pepper as needed
- Cayenne pepper as needed

1. Halve the avocados and discard the stone.
2. Scoop flesh from 3 avocado halves and transfer to a large bowl.
3. Mash using fork.
4. Add 2 tablespoon of lime juice and mix.
5. Dice the remaining avocado flesh (remaining half) and transfer to another bowl
6. Add remaining juice and toss.
7. Add diced flesh with the mashed flesh and mix.
8. Add chopped onions and toss.
9. Season with salt, pepper, and cayenne pepper.
10. Serve and enjoy!

PER SERVING

Calories: 172 Fat: 15 g Saturated Fat: 2 g Carbohydrates: 11 g Fiber: 2 g Sodium: 279 mg Protein: 16 g

Coconut Porridge

Prep time: 10 minutes | Cook time:5 minutes | Serves 3

- 2 cups of water
- 1 cup coconut cream
- ½ cup unsweetened dried and shredded coconut
- 2 tablespoons flaxseed meal
- 1 tablespoon vegan butter
- 1 and ½ teaspoon stevia
- 1 teaspoon cinnamon
- Salt to taste
- Toppings such as blueberries

1. Add the listed ingredients to a small pot, mix well.
2. Transfer pot to stove and place it over medium-low heat.
3. Bring to mix to a slow boil.
4. Stir well and remove from the heat.
5. Divide the mix into equal servings and let them sit for 10 minutes.
6. Top with your desired toppings, and enjoy!

PER SERVING

Calories: 171 Fat: 16 g Carbohydrate: 6 g Protein: 2 g Saturated Fat: 4 g Fiber: 2 g Sodium: 246 mg

One-Skillet Kale and Avocado

Prep time: 10 minutes | Cook time: 0 minutes | Serves 3

- 2 tablespoons olive oil, divided
- 2 cups sliced mushrooms
- 5 ounces fresh kale, stemmed and sliced into ribbons
- 1 avocado, sliced
- 4 large whole eggs
- Salt and pepper as needed

1. Take a large skillet and place it over medium heat.
2. Add a tablespoon of olive oil.
3. Add mushrooms to the pan and Sauté for 3 minutes.
4. Take a medium bowl and massage kale with the remaining 1 tablespoon olive oil (for about 1-2 minutes).
5. Add kale to skillet and place them on top of mushrooms.
6. Place slices of avocado on top of the kale.
7. Create 4 wells for eggs and crack an egg onto each well.
8. Season eggs with salt and pepper.
9. Cover skillet and cook for 5 minutes.
10. Serve hot!

PER SERVING

Calories: 461 Fat: 34 g
Carbohydrate: 6 g Protein: 18 g Saturated Fat: 12 g
Fiber: 2 g Sodium: 250 mg

Grilled Zucchini Meal

Prep time: 10 minutes | Cook time: 60 minutes | Serves 3

- Olive oil as needed
- 3 zucchinis
- ½ teaspoon black pepper
- ½ teaspoon mustard
- ½ teaspoon cumin
- 1 teaspoon paprika
- 1 teaspoon garlic powder
- 1 tablespoon sea salt
- 1-2 stevia
- 1 tablespoon chili powder

1. Preheat your oven to 300 degrees F.
2. Take a small bowl and add cayenne, black pepper, salt, garlic, mustard, paprika, chili powder, and stevia.
3. Mix well.
4. Slice zucchini into 1/8 inch slices and spray them with olive oil.
5. Sprinkle spice blend over Zucchini and bake for 40 minutes.
6. Remove and flip, spray with more olive oil and leftover spice.
7. Bake for 20 minutes more.
8. Serve!

PER SERVING

Calories: 95 Fat: 7 g
Carbohydrate: 4 g Protein: 1 g Saturated Fat: 2 g Fiber: 1 g Sodium: 285 mg

Authentic Mushroom and Beet Salsa

Prep time: 10 minutes | Cook time: 20 minutes | Serves 4

- 4 medium Portobello mushroom caps,
- ¼ cup lemon juice
- 3 tablespoons olive oil
- 1 small shallot, chopped
- 5 ounces baby kale
- 8 ounces precooked, chopped beets
- 2 thinly sliced, ripe avocados

1. Take a large-sized rimmed baking sheet and spray the Portobello mushroom caps with cooking spray.
2. Sprinkle ½ teaspoon of salt.
3. Add mushrooms to the baking sheet and bake for 20 minutes at 450 degrees Fahrenheit.
4. Take a bowl and whisk in lemon juice, shallot, olive oil, ¼ teaspoon of salt, ¼ teaspoon of pepper.
5. Add half of the beets and baby kale, toss them well.
6. Divide the mixture amongst serving plates and top them with mushrooms and avocado.
7. Serve with the dressing and enjoy!

PER SERVING

Calories: 370 Fat: 26 g Saturated Fat: 4 g Carbohydrates: 32 g Fiber: 3 g Sodium: 393 mg Protein: 7 g

Hearty Oatmeal Muffins

Prep time: 10 minutes | Cook time:15 minutes | Serves 12

- 2 cups peeled and chopped apple
- 1 and a ½ cups all-purpose flour
- 1 cup of quick-cooking oats
- 2/3 cup of brown sugar, firmly packed
- 1 and a ½ teaspoon baking powder
- ½ a teaspoon baking soda
- ½ a teaspoon salt
- ½ a teaspoon ground cinnamon
- ½ a cup vegan suitable milk
- 2 tablespoon vegetable oil

1. Preheat your oven to 375 degrees Fahrenheit.
2. Take 12 muffin cups and line them with paper liners.
3. Take a bowl and add flour, oats, brown sugar, baking soda, baking powder, salt, milk, cinnamon, and oil.
4. Mix well until the batter forms.
5. Divide the batter between the muffin cups.
6. Bake for 15-18 minutes until a toothpick comes out clean.
7. Serve and enjoy!

PER SERVING

Calories: 167 Fat: 3g Carbohydrates: 32g Protein: 3g Saturated Fat: 1g Fiber: 5g Sodium: 333g

Sliced Up Apple Fires

Prep time: 10 minutes | Cook time:10 minutes | Serves 4

- ½ cup coconut oil
- ¼ cup date paste
- 2 tablespoons ground cinnamon
- 4 Granny Smith apples, peeled, cored, and sliced

1. Take a medium-sized skillet and place it over medium heat.
2. Add oil and allow the oil to heat up.
3. Stir in cinnamon and date paste into the oil.
4. Add sliced apples and cook for 5 to 8 minutes until crispy.
5. Enjoy!

PER SERVING

Calories: 368 Fat: 23 g Saturated Fat: 10 g Carbohydrates: 44 g Fiber: 12 g Sodium: 182 mg Protein: 1 g

The Low Carb Cream of Mushroom Soup

Prep time: 10 minutes | Cook time:30 minutes | Serves 3

- 1 tablespoon olive oil
- ½ large onion, diced
- 20 ounces mushrooms, sliced
- 6 garlic cloves, minced
- 2 cups vegetable broth
- 1 cup coconut cream

- ¾ teaspoon salt
- ¼ teaspoon black pepper

1. Take a medium-sized pot and place it over medium heat.
2. Add onion and mushrooms in olive oil and Sauté for 10-15 minutes.
3. Make sure to keep stirring it from time to time until it browned evenly.
4. Add garlic and sauté for 1 minute more.
5. Add vegetable broth, coconut cream, black pepper, and salt.
6. Bring it to a boil and reduce the temperature to low.
7. Simmer for 15 minutes.
8. Use an immersion blender to puree the mixture.
9. Enjoy!

PER SERVING

Calories: 200 Fat: 17 g Saturated Fat: 3 g Carbohydrates: 5 g Fiber: 2 g Sodium: 427 mg Protein: 4 g

Superb Kale and Spinach Bowl

Prep time: 10 minutes | Cook time:10 minutes | Serves 3

- 3 ounces coconut oil
- 8 ounces kale, chopped
- 2 avocado, diced
- 4 and 1/3 cups coconut milk
- Salt and pepper to taste

1. Take a skillet and place it over medium heat.
2. Add kale and sauté for 2-3 minutes.
3. Add kale to the blender.
4. Add coconut milk, and avocado to the blender as well.
5. Blend until smooth and pour the mix into a bowl.
6. Serve and enjoy!

PER SERVING

Calories: 7 Fat: 13 g Saturated Fat: 2 g Carbohydrates: 7 g Fiber: 1 g Sodium: 247 mg Protein: 5 g

Classic Lentil Soup with Swiss Chard

Prep time: 10 minutes| Cook time: 25 minutes| Serves 5

- 2 tablespoons olive oil
- 1 white onion, chopped
- 1 teaspoon garlic, minced
- 2 large carrots, chopped
- 1 parsnip, chopped
- 2 stalks celery, chopped
- 2 bay leaves
- 1/2 teaspoon dried thyme
- 1/4 teaspoon ground cumin
- 5 cups roasted vegetable broth
- 1 ¼ cups brown lentils, soaked overnight and rinsed
- 2 cups Swiss chard, torn into pieces

1. In a heavy-bottomed pot, heat the olive oil over a moderate heat. Now, sauté the vegetables along with the spices for about 3 minutes until they are just tender.
2. Add in the vegetable broth and lentils, bringing it to a boil. Immediately turn the heat to a simmer and add in the bay leaves. Let it cook for about 15 minutes or until lentils are tender.
3. Add in the Swiss chard, cover and let it simmer for 5 minutes more or until the chard wilts.
4. Serve in individual bowls and enjoy!

PER SERVING

Calories: 148; Fat: 7.2g; Carbs: 14.6g; Protein: 7.7g

Cannellini Bean Soup with Kale

Prep time: 10 minutes| Cook time: 25 minutes| Serves 5

- 1 tablespoon olive oil
- 1/2 teaspoon ginger, minced
- 1/2 teaspoon cumin seeds
- 1 red onion, chopped
- 1 carrot, trimmed and chopped
- 1 parsnip, trimmed and chopped
- 2 garlic cloves, minced
- 5 cups vegetable broth
- 12 ounces cannellini beans, drained
- 2 cups kale, torn into pieces
- Sea salt and ground black pepper, to taste

1. In a heavy-bottomed pot, heat the olive over medium-high heat. Now, sauté the ginger and cumin for 1 minute or so.
2. Now, add in the onion, carrot and parsnip; continue sautéing an additional 3 minutes or until the vegetables are just tender.
3. Add in the garlic and continue to sauté for 1 minute or until aromatic.
4. Then, pour in the vegetable broth and bring to a boil. Immediately reduce the heat to a simmer and let it cook for 10 minutes.
5. Fold in the Cannellini beans and kale; continue to simmer until the kale wilts and everything is thoroughly heated. Season with salt and pepper

to taste.
6. Ladle into individual bowls and serve hot. Bon appétit!

PER SERVING

Calories: 188; Fat: 4.7g; Carbs: 24.5g; Protein: 11.1g

Spicy Winter Farro Soup

Prep time: 10 minutes| Cook time: 30 minutes| Serves 4

- 2 tablespoons olive oil
- 1 medium-sized leek, chopped
- 1 medium-sized turnip, sliced
- 2 Italian peppers, seeded and chopped
- 1 jalapeno pepper, minced
- 2 potatoes, peeled and diced
- 4 cups vegetable broth
- 1 cup farro, rinsed
- 1/2 teaspoon granulated garlic
- 1/2 teaspoon turmeric powder
- 1 bay laurel
- 2 cups spinach, turn into pieces

1. In a heavy-bottomed pot, heat the olive oil over a moderate heat. Now, sauté the leek, turnip, peppers and potatoes for about 5 minutes until they are crisp-tender.
2. Add in the vegetable broth, farro, granulated garlic, turmeric and bay laurel; bring it to a boil.
3. Immediately turn the heat to a simmer. Let it cook for about 25 minutes or until farro and potatoes have softened.
4. Add in the spinach and remove the pot from the heat; let the spinach sit in the residual heat until it wilts. Bon appétit!

PER SERVING

Calories: 298; Fat: 8.9g; Carbs: 44.6g; Protein: 11.7g

Tomato Soup

Prep time: 10 minutes| Cook time: 10 minutes| Serves 2

- 56 ounces stewed tomatoes
- ¼ teaspoon salt
- ¼ teaspoon ground black pepper
- 1 medium red bell pepper, cored, diced
- ¼ teaspoon dried thyme
- 6 leaves of basil, chopped
- ¼ teaspoon dried oregano
- 1 teaspoon olive oil

1. Take a medium pot, place it over medium heat, add oil, and when hot, add bell pepper and then cook for 4 minutes.
2. Add remaining ingredients into the pot, stir until mixed, switch heat to medium-high heat, and bring the mixture to simmer.
3. Remove pot from the heat and then puree the soup until smooth.
4. Taste to adjust seasoning, ladle soup into bowls and then serve.

PER SERVING

Calories: 170 Cal; Fat: 1.1 g; Protein: 3.5 g; Carbs: 36 g; Fiber: 2.6 g

Hearty Winter Quinoa Soup

Prep time: 10 minutes| Cook time: 25 minutes| Serves 4

- 2 tablespoons olive oil
- 1 onion, chopped
- 2 carrots, peeled and chopped
- 1 parsnip, chopped
- 1 celery stalk, chopped
- 1 cup yellow squash, chopped
- 4 garlic cloves, pressed or minced
- 4 cups roasted vegetable broth
- 2 medium tomatoes, crushed
- 1 cup quinoa
- Sea salt and ground black pepper, to taste
- 1 bay laurel
- 2 cup Swiss chard, tough ribs removed and torn into pieces
- 2 tablespoons Italian parsley, chopped

1. In a heavy-bottomed pot, heat the olive over medium-high heat. Now, sauté the onion, carrot, parsnip, celery and yellow squash for about 3 minutes or until the vegetables are just tender.
2. Add in the garlic and continue to sauté for 1 minute or until aromatic.
3. Then, stir in the vegetable broth, tomatoes, quinoa, salt, pepper and bay laurel; bring to a boil. Immediately reduce the heat to a simmer and let it cook for 13 minutes.
4. Fold in the Swiss chard; continue to simmer until the chard wilts.
5. Ladle into individual bowls and serve garnished with the fresh parsley. Bon appétit!

PER SERVING

Calories: 328; Fat: 11.1g; Carbs: 44.1g; Protein: 13.3g

Rainbow Chickpea Salad

Prep time: 15 minutes| Cook time: 0 minutes| Serves 4

- 16 ounces canned chickpeas, drained
- 1 medium avocado, sliced
- 1 bell pepper, seeded and sliced
- 1 large tomato, sliced
- 2 cucumbers, diced
- 1 red onion, sliced
- 1/2 teaspoon garlic, minced
- 1/4 cup fresh parsley, chopped
- 1/4 cup olive oil
- 2 tablespoons apple cider vinegar
- 1/2 lime, freshly squeezed
- Sea salt and ground black pepper, to taste

1. Toss all the Ingredients in a salad bowl.
2. Place the salad in your refrigerator for about 1 hour before serving.
3. Bonappétit!

PER SERVING

Calories: 378; Fat: 24g; Carbs: 34.2g; Protein: 10.1g

Roasted Asparagus and Avocado Salad

Prep time: 10 minutes| Cook time: 15 minutes| Serves 4

- 1-pound asparagus, trimmed, cut into bite-sized pieces
- 1 white onion, chopped
- 2 garlic cloves, minced
- 1 Roma tomato, sliced
- 1/4 cup olive oil
- 1/4 cup balsamic vinegar
- 1 tablespoon stone-ground mustard
- 2 tablespoons fresh parsley, chopped
- 1 tablespoon fresh cilantro, chopped
- 1 tablespoon fresh basil, chopped
- Sea salt and ground black pepper, to taste
- 1 small avocado, pitted and diced
- 1/2 cup pine nuts, roughly chopped

1. Begin by preheating your oven to 420 degrees F.
2. Toss the asparagus with 1 tablespoon of the olive oil and arrange them on a parchment-lined roasting pan.
3. Bake for about 15 minutes, rotating the pan once or twice to promote even cooking. Let it cool completely and place in your salad bowl.
4. Toss the asparagus with the vegetables, olive oil, vinegar, mustard and herbs. Salt and pepper to taste.
5. Toss to combine and top with avocado and pine nuts. Bon appétit!

PER SERVING

Calories: 378; Fat: 33.2g; Carbs: 18.6g; Protein: 7.8g

Creamed Pinto Bean Salad with Pine Nuts

Prep time: 10 minutes| Cook time: 5 minutes| Serves 5

- 1 ½ pounds pinto beans, trimmed
- 2 medium tomatoes, diced
- 2 bell peppers, seeded and diced
- 4 tablespoons shallots, chopped
- 1/2 cup pine nuts, roughly chopped
- 1/2 cup vegan mayonnaise
- 1 tablespoon deli mustard
- 2 tablespoons fresh basil, chopped
- 2 tablespoons fresh parsley, chopped
- 1/2 teaspoon red pepper flakes, crushed
- Sea salt and freshly ground black pepper, to taste

1. Boil the pinto beans in a large saucepan of salted water until they are just tender or about 2 minutes.
2. Drain and let the beans cool completely; then, transfer them to a salad bowl. Toss the beans with the remaining ingredients.
3. Taste and adjust the seasonings. Bon appétit!

PER SERVING

Calories: 308; Fat: 26.2g; Carbs: 16.6g; Protein: 5.8g

Hearty Cream of Mushroom Soup

Prep time: 10 minutes| Cook time: 15 minutes| Serves 5

- 2 tablespoons soy butter
- 1 large shallot, chopped
- 20 ounces Cremini mushrooms, sliced
- 2 cloves garlic, minced
- 4 tablespoons flaxseed meal
- 5 cups vegetable broth
- 1 1/3 cups full-fat coconut milk
- 1 bay leaf
- Sea salt and ground black pepper, to taste

1. In a stockpot, melt the vegan butter over medium-high heat. Once hot, cook the shallot for about 3 minutes until tender and fragrant.
2. Add in the mushrooms and garlic and continue cooking until the mushrooms have softened. Add in the flaxseed meal and continue to cook for 1 minute or so.
3. Add in the remaining ingredients. Let it simmer, covered and continue to cook for 5 to 6 minutes more until your soup has thickened slightly.
4. Bon appétit!

PER SERVING

Calories: 308; Fat: 25.5g; Carbs: 11.8g; Protein: 11.6g

Authentic Italian Panzanella Salad

Prep time: 10 minutes| Cook time: 35 minutes| Serves 3

- 3 cups artisan bread, broken into 1-inch cubes
- 3/4-pound asparagus, trimmed and cut into bite-sized pieces
- 4 tablespoons extra-virgin olive oil
- 1 red onion, chopped
- 2 tablespoons fresh lime juice
- 1 teaspoon deli mustard
- 2 medium heirloom tomatoes, diced
- 2 cups arugula
- 2 cups baby spinach
- 2 Italian peppers, seeded and sliced
- Sea salt and ground black pepper, to taste

1. Arrange the bread cubes on a parchment-lined baking sheet. Bake in the preheated oven at 310 degrees F for about 20 minutes, rotating the baking sheet twice during the baking time; reserve.
2. Turn the oven to 420 degrees F and toss the asparagus with 1 tablespoon of olive oil. Roast the asparagus for about 15 minutes or until crisp-tender.
3. Toss the remaining Ingredients in a salad bowl; top with the roasted asparagus and toasted bread.
4. Bon!

PER SERVING

Calories: 334; Fat: 20.4g; Carbs: 33.3g; Protein: 8.3g

Quinoa and Black Bean Salad

Prep time: 10 minutes| Cook time: 15 minutes + chilling time| Serves 4

- 2 cups water
- 1 cup quinoa, rinsed
- 16 ounces canned black beans, drained
- 2 Roma tomatoes, sliced
- 1 red onion, thinly sliced
- 1 cucumber, seeded and chopped
- 2 cloves garlic, pressed or minced
- 2 Italian peppers, seeded and sliced
- 2 tablespoons fresh parsley, chopped
- 2 tablespoons fresh cilantro, chopped
- 1/4 cup olive oil
- 1 lemon, freshly squeezed
- 1 tablespoon apple cider vinegar
- 1/2 teaspoon dried dill weed
- 1/2 teaspoon dried oregano
- Sea salt and ground black pepper, to taste

1. Place the water and quinoa in a saucepan and bring it to a rolling boil. Immediately turn the heat to a simmer.
2. Let it simmer for about 13 minutes until the quinoa has absorbed all of the water; fluff the quinoa with a fork and let it cool completely. Then, transfer the quinoa to a salad bowl.
3. Add the remaining Ingredients to the salad bowl and toss to combine well. Bon appétit!

PER SERVING

Calories: 433; Fat: 17.3g; Carbs: 57g; Protein: 15.1g

Rich Bulgur Salad with Herbs

Prep time: 10 minutes| Cook time: 20 minutes + chilling time| Serves 4

- 2 cups water
- 1 cup bulgur
- 12 ounces canned chickpeas, drained
- 1 Persian cucumber, thinly sliced
- 2 bell peppers, seeded and thinly sliced
- 1 jalapeno pepper, seeded and thinly sliced
- 2 Roma tomatoes, sliced
- 1 onion, thinly sliced
- 2 tablespoons fresh basil, chopped
- 2 tablespoons fresh parsley, chopped
- 2 tablespoons fresh mint, chopped
- 2 tablespoons fresh chives, chopped
- 4 tablespoons olive oil
- 1 tablespoon balsamic vinegar
- 1 tablespoon lemon juice
- 1 teaspoon fresh garlic, pressed
- Sea salt and freshly ground black pepper, to taste
- 2 tablespoons nutritional yeast
- 1/2 cup Kalamata olives, sliced

1. In a saucepan, bring the water and bulgur to a boil. Immediately turn the heat to a simmer and let it cook for about 20 minutes or until the bulgur is tender and water is almost absorbed. Fluff with a fork and spread on a large tray to let cool.
2. Place the bulgur in a salad bowl followed by the chickpeas, cucumber, peppers, tomatoes, onion, basil, parsley, mint and chives.
3. In a small mixing dish, whisk the olive oil, balsamic vinegar, lemon juice, garlic, salt and black pepper. Dress the salad and toss to combine.
4. Sprinkle nutritional yeast over the top, garnish with olives and serve at room temperature. Bon appétit!

PER SERVING

Calories: 408; Fat: 18.3g; Carbs: 51.8g; Protein: 13.1g

Classic Roasted Pepper Salad

Prep time: 10 minutes| Cook time: 15 minutes + chilling time| Serves 3

- 6 bell peppers
- 3 tablespoons extra-virgin olive oil
- 3 teaspoons red wine vinegar
- 3 garlic cloves, finely chopped
- 2 tablespoons fresh parsley, chopped
- Sea salt and freshly cracked black pepper, to taste
- 1/2 teaspoon red pepper flakes
- 6 tablespoons pine nuts, roughly chopped

1. Broil the peppers on a parchment-lined baking sheet for about 10 minutes, rotating the pan halfway through the cooking time, until they are charred on all sides.
2. Then, cover the peppers with a plastic wrap to steam. Discard the skin, seeds and cores.
3. Slice the peppers into strips and toss them with

the remaining ingredients. Place in your refrigerator until ready to serve. Bon appétit!

PER SERVING

Calories: 178; Fat: 14.4g; Carbs: 11.8g; Protein: 2.4g

Scallion Bacon Chicken Salad

Prep time: 15 minutes | Cook time: 20 minutes | Serves 5

- 1/2 tsp. of garlic powder
- 1 lb. of skinless, boneless chicken breasts
- 1/2 tsp. of onion powder
- 8 slices of bacon (uncured), sugar-free
- Sea salt & black pepper, to taste
- 3 scallions, thinly sliced (green onions)
- 1/2 cup of homemade vegan mayo

1. Slice the bacon into bite-sized pieces and cook it in a large pan over medium-high heat until it is crisp.
2. While keeping the reduced fat in the pan, remove the bacon from the skillet and put it aside to drain it on paper towels.
3. The chicken breasts should be pounded to a thickness of 1/2 inch or sliced in half so that each piece is half inch thick.
4. Reduce the heat to medium. Place the chicken breasts in the bacon fat-coated skillet after liberally seasoning them with salt, pepper, garlic powder, and onion powder. If you would like, use refined coconut oil or ghee. Cook for two to three minutes on each side, or till the inside is not pink anymore.
5. Place the chicken into a large bowl, cover, and chill in the fridge. Now is the perfect time to make mayo if you haven't already.
6. Once the chicken has cooled, shred or roughly cut it into bite-sized pieces and combine with the scallions, bacon, and mayonnaise in a large bowl. Mix everything well.
7. If necessary, taste & add salt or pepper. Immediately serve, or cover and store for later. In a container that is well closed, the chicken salad may be stored in the fridge for 3–4 days. Enjoy!

PER SERVING

Total Calories: 420kcal, Fats: 34g, Carbohydrates: 0g, Protein: 25g, Fiber: 0g, Sodium: 420mg, Potassium: 422mg

Taco Grilled Chicken Salad

Prep time: 30 minutes | Cook time: 20 minutes | Serves 4

- ¾ cup of medium-hot salsa
- 1 can of black beans (15 ounces), rinsed & drained
- ½ cup of chopped fresh cilantro
- 2 tbsp. of chili powder
- 1 tbsp. of lime juice
- 1 tsp. of ground cumin
- 1 tsp. of brown sugar
- 1 tsp. of ground coriander
- ¼ tsp. of cayenne pepper
- 1 pound of boneless, skinless chicken breast halves
- 1 tbsp. of olive oil
- 4 corn tortillas (7 inches)
- ½ cup of chopped fresh cilantro
- 4 cups of shredded lettuce
- 1 peeled avocado, pitted & sliced (Optional)
- ¼ cup of sour cream (Optional)
- 1 lime, cut in wedges (Optional)

1. Set an outside grill over medium-high heat and give the grates quick oiling.
2. In a bowl, combine the black beans, salsa, half the cilantro, and lime juice.
3. Rub the mixture on chicken breasts by combining chili powder, coriander, cumin, brown sugar, olive oil , and cayenne pepper in a bowl.
4. Cook the chicken breasts on a hot grill for 10 to 12 minutes on each side or until juices run clear and the center is no longer pink. In the middle, an instant-read thermometer should register at least 165 degrees Fahrenheit (74 degrees C). Place the tortillas on the grill and cook them for 3 to 5 minutes, or until they are just beginning to gently brown on both sides.
5. Slice the chicken into long, thin strips after transferring it to a chopping board. On top of the tortillas, distribute the chicken strips, the bean mixture, the lettuce, and the last 1/2 cup of cilantro. Serve with avocado, sour cream, and lime wedges.

PER SERVING

Total Calories: 470kcal, Fats: 18.7g, Carbohydrates: 44.4g, Protein: 35.2g, Fiber: 15.9g, Sodium: 831.8mg, Potassium: 1215.1mg

Breakfast Salad

Prep time: 10 minutes | Cook time: 10 minutes | Serves 4

- 1/3 chopped shallot or red onion
- 1 1/3 cup of butternut squash, chopped and peeled
- 1 1/2 tbsp. of butter or olive oil (divided)
- 1 tbsp. of balsamic vinegar
- 12 ounces of mixture broccoli coleslaw salad
- 1 tbsp. of water
- 1/4 tsp. or more of sea salt & pepper each (to taste)
- 1/4 tsp. of garlic, minced
- 1/3 cup of blueberries
- Red pepper flakes & cilantro for garnishing
- 4 eggs
- Roasted pumpkin seeds
- 1 sliced avocado

1. Peel and cut your vegetables first. If you don't want to wait until the end, slice your avocado. Put the chopped squash and 1 tablespoon of water in a steamer over a microwave-safe plate. Steam for at least 2 and a half minutes based on the power of the microwave. Cook until mushy but still firm. Alternately, roast the squash on a baking sheet for 15 to 20 minutes at 425F.
2. Eliminate, drain, and reserve. Put 1 tablespoon of butter or oil in a small skillet. Add your onions and turn the heat to medium-high.
3. Fry onions for two minutes or until they begin to color slightly. Then add your slaw, garlic, salt, and pepper, along with 1 tablespoon of water and balsamic vinegar.
4. Combine everything in a skillet. For two to three minutes on medium, cook covered.
5. Slaw won't be entirely cooked but will be just slightly tender. Take it out and put it in a bowl.
6. Toss the squash & 1/3 cup of berries into the bowl. Eggs are then cooked in same skillet. On medium-high heat, add another half tbsp of butter or oil.
7. Fry until the yolk is set and the exterior is crispy. Based on how you want your yolk, cook it for 3 to 4 minutes or less. Place slaw on three to four plates or bowls.
8. Fry an egg and place it on each. Add red pepper, one tablespoon of cilantro, pumpkin seeds, and any additional salt or pepper to garnish. Serve with sliced avocado.

PER SERVING

Total Calories: 235kcal, Fats: 15.3g, Carbohydrates: 18.8g, Protein: 9.2g, Fiber: 7g, Sodium: 213.1mg, Potassium: 0mg

Easy Salad

Prep time:10 minutes | Cook time:0 minutes | Serves 4

- ½ cup banana, peeled and sliced
- ½ cup kiwi, peeled and chopped
- ½ cup fresh strawberries, hulled and sliced
- ¼ cup seedless red grapes, halved
- ¼ cup seedless green grapes, halved
- ½ cup apple, cored and chopped
- 2 tablespoons extra virgin olive oil or coconut oil
- 2 tablespoons fresh lemon juice
- Salt and freshly ground black pepper, to taste
- 4 cups fresh baby spinach

1. In a large salad bowl, add all ingredients except baby spinach and toss to coat well.
2. Serve immediately over the bed of baby spinach.

PER SERVING

Calories: 123Fat: 7.4gSodium: 27mg Carbohydrates: 14.8gFiber: 2.7g Sugar: 9.3g Protein: 1.7g

Lovely Orange Salad

Prep time: 10 minutes | Cook time:0 minutes | Serves 3

- 6 large orange
- 3 tablespoon red wine vinegar
- 6 tablespoon olive oil
- 1 teaspoon dried oregano
- 1 red onion, thinly sliced
- 1 cup olive oil
- ¼ cup fresh chives, chopped
- Ground black pepper

1. Peel the orange and cut each of them into 4-5 crosswise slices.
2. Transfer the oranges to a shallow dish.
3. Drizzle vinegar, olive oil, and sprinkle oregano.
4. Toss.
5. Chill for 30 minutes.
6. Arrange sliced onion and black olives on top.
7. Decorate with an additional sprinkle of chives and a fresh grind of pepper.
8. Serve and enjoy!

PER SERVING

Calories: 120 Fat: 6g Carbohydrates: 20g Protein: 2g Saturated Fat:5g Fiber: 5g Sodium: 392 mg

Almond and Tomato Salad

Prep time: 15 minutes| Cook time: 10 minutes| Serves 4

- 1 cup arugula/ rocket
- 7 oz fresh tomatoes, sliced or chopped
- 2 teaspoons olive oil
- 2 cups kale
- 1/2 cup almonds

1. Put oil into your pan and heat it on a medium heat. Add tomatoes into the pan and fry for about 10 minutes. Once cooked, allow it to cool. Combine all salad ingredients in a bowl and serve.

PER SERVING

Calories: 355 Fat 19.1 g Carbohydrate 8.3 g Protein 33 g

Strawberry Spinach Salad

Prep time: 15 minutes| Cook time: 0 minutes| Serves 4

- 5 cups baby spinach
- 2 cups strawberries, sliced
- 2 tablespoons lemon juice
- 1/2 teaspoon Dijon mustard
- 1/4 cup olive oil
- 3/4 cup toasted almonds, chopped
- 1/4 red onion, sliced
- Salt, pepper, to taste

1. Take a large bowl and mix Dijon mustard with lemon juice in it, and slowly add olive oil and combine. Season the mixture with black pepper and salt.
2. Now, mix strawberries, half cup of almonds, and sliced onion in a bowl. Pour the dressing on top and toss to combine. Serve the salad topped with almonds and vegan cheese.

PER SERVING

Calories: 116Fat 3 g Carbs 13 g Protein 6 g

Dried Apple Rings

Prep time: 20 minutes| Cook time: 5 hours | Serves 4-6

- 3 pounds of peeled apples, cut into 0.1-inches of rings
- 1 teaspoon of salt
- 1.7ounces of lemon juice

1. In a bowl, add 3 cups of water, lemon juice and salt. Mix well.
2. Add the rings to the lemon water, let it rest for ten minutes.
3. Take the rings out and drain them on a paper towel.
4. Lay 2 layers of cheesecloth on a cooling rack, place the slices on top and place the rack on the cooking grate.
5. Place the entire set up in the cold oven at 125 F. As the temperature reaches, keep the oven door open slightly.
6. Change the temperature to 150 F.
7. Let the apples dry for 5 hours, with the door slightly open. Cool completely before serving.

PER SERVING

Calories: 21 Total fat: 0 g Total carbs: 2 g Fiber: 2 g Sugar: 3.2 g Protein: 0 g Sodium: 45 mg

Chickpea Medley

Prep time: 5minutes | Cook time: 0 minutes | Serves 4

- 2 tablespoons tahini
- 2 tablespoons coconut amines
- 1 (15-ounce) can chickpeas or 1.1/2 cups cooked chickpeas, rinsed and drained
- 1 cup finely chopped lightly packed spinach
- carrot, peeled and grated

1. Merge together the tahini and coconut amines in a bowl.
2. Add the chickpeas, spinach, and carrot to the bowl. Stir well and serve at room temperature.
3. Simple Swap: Coconut amines are almost like a sweeter, mellower version of soy sauce. However, if you want to use regular soy sauce or tamari, just use 11/2 tablespoons and add a dash of maple syrup or agave nectar to balance out the saltiness.

PER SERVING

Calories: 437 Total fat: 8g Protein: 92g Sodium: 246 Fat: 19g

Roasted Pine Nut Orzo

Prep time: 10minutes | Cook time: 15minutes | Serves 3

- 16 ounces' orzo
- 1 cup diced roasted red peppers
- 1/4 cup pitted, chopped Klamath olives
- 4 garlic cloves, minced or pressed
- 3 tablespoons olive oil
- 1.1/2 tablespoons squeezed lemon juice

- 2 teaspoons balsamic vinegar
- 1 teaspoon sea salt
- 1/4 cup pine nuts
- 1/4 cup packed thinly sliced or torn fresh basil

1. Use a large pot of water to a boil over medium-high heat and add the orzo. Cook, stirring often, for 10 minutes, or until the orzo has a chewy and firm texture. Drain well.
2. While the orzo is cooking, in a large bowl, combine the peppers, olives, garlic, olive oil, lemon juice, vinegar, and salt. Stir well.
3. In a dry skillet toasts the pine nuts over medium-low heat until aromatic and lightly browned, shaking the pan often so that they cook evenly
4. Upon reaching the desired texture and add it to the sauce mixture within a minute or so, to avoid clumping.

PER SERVING

Calories: 423 Total fat: 4g Protein: 64g Sodium: 231 Fat: 12g

Banana and Almond Butter Oats

Prep time: 10 minutes| Cook time: 5 minutes| Serves 2

- 1 cup gluten-free moved oats
- 1 cup almond milk
- 1 cup of water
- 1 teaspoon cinnamon
- 2 tablespoons almond spread
- 1 banana, cut

1. Mix the water and almond milk to a bubble in a little pot. Add the oats and diminish to a stew.
2. Cook until oats have consumed all fluid. Blend in cinnamon. Top with almond spread and banana and serve.

PER SERVING

Calories: 112, Fat: 10g Protein: 9g Carbohydrates: 54g

Chicken & Mushroom Skewers

Prep time: 20 minutes| Cook time: 10 minutes| Serves 4-6

- 4 oz. of button mushroom
- Half teaspoon olive oil
- Half bunch of cilantro
- 1 red chili pepper
- Salt, to taste
- 3 oz. of chicken breasts

1. Chop the chili without seeds.
2. Onto soaked skewers, thread the mushrooms and chicken pieces alternatively. Season with salt.
3. In a pan, add oil and chilies, cook the skewers until golden brown. Serve with cilantro on top.

PER SERVING

Calories: 176 Total fat: 4.3 g Total carbs: 4 g Fiber: 1.8 g Sugar: 3 g Protein:21 g Sodium: 155 mg

Peas & Pancetta

Prep time: 10 minutes| Cook time: 10 minutes| Serves 4

- 2 oz. of cooked pancetta
- ¼ cup of dry white wine
- 3 tablespoons of chopped onion
- Salt & pepper to taste
- 1 pound of peas
- 2 tablespoons of olive oil
- 1 ½ tablespoon of fresh thyme, chopped

1. In a pan, cook onion and pancetta in hot oil for 5 minutes.
2. Add the rest of the ingredients, stir well.
3. Let it come to a boil, turn the heat low and simmer for 3-5 minutes.
4. Serve.

PER SERVING

Calories: 189 Total fat: 9.1 g Total carbs: 17 g Fiber: 3 g Sugar: 3 g Protein: 7.7 g Sodium: 232.2 mg

Green Beans Almondine

Prep time: 10 minutes| Cook time: 10 minutes| Serves 4

1. 1/4 cup of slivered almonds
2. 1 tablespoon of minced garlic
3. Half teaspoon of Salt & pepper
4. 1 lb. of trimmed green beans
5. 2 tablespoons of olive oil
6. 2 tablespoons of water

7. In a pan, heat oil on medium flame.
8. Sauté garlic for 1 minute. Add beans with salt and pepper, cook for 2 minutes.
9. Add water, cover, and cook for 5 minutes.
10. Take the lid off and add almonds; cook for 1 to 2 minutes.

PER SERVING

Calories: 139 Total fat: 11 g Total carbs: 10 g Fiber: 4 g Sugar: 4 g Protein: 4 g Sodium: 298 mg

Paleo Ginger Garlic Zoodles

Prep time: 10 minutes| Cook time: 20 minutes| Serves 2

- 1/4 cup of coconut oil
- 1 tablespoon of grated ginger
- 4 zucchinis, spiralized
- minced garlic cloves
- 2 cups of broccoli florets
- 1 tablespoon of maple syrup
- Half teaspoon of sea salt
- 1 cup of cauliflower florets
- black pepper, to taste
- 3 tablespoons of coconut aminos
- 1/4 cup sliced green onions

1. In a skillet, add zoodles, garlic, ginger, oil and salt; cook for 5 to 10 minutes.
2. Do not overcook or mush the zoodles.
3. Add cauliflower, broccoli, maple syrup and coconut aminos. Cook for 2 to 5 minutes, covered.
4. Turn the heat off and let it rest for few minutes. Serve with black pepper and green onion on top.

PER SERVING

Calories: 216 Total fat: 6 g Total carbs: 4 g Fiber: 7 g Sugar: 3 g Protein: 3 g Sodium: 121 mg

Sweet Potato Hash & Fried Eggs

Prep time: 10 minutes | Cook time: 15 minutes | Serves 2

For hash:
- 1 large pinch of kosher salt
- 1 garnet yam (large)
- Black pepper, freshly ground
- Some dashes of onion powder
- Some garlic powder
- Dried herbs, a small sprinkle
- Aleppo pepper (optional)
- 2 tbsp. of fat (any)

For eggs:
- 1 tbsp. of avocado oil or ghee
- 4 eggs (large), two per serving
- Kosher salt
- Aleppo pepper (optional)
- Black pepper, freshly ground

1. Based on how many people you'll be serving, grab one or seven yams.
2. In order for the yam slices to fit in your food processor, peel and chop them lengthwise. Shred the yams using the slicer blade attached to the machine. (Alternatively, you may create sweet potato "noodles" with a spiralizer.)
3. Toss the shredded yams with salt, pepper, garlic powder, onion powder, and dry herbs in a large bowl. If you have fresh alliums and herbs, you can surely use them instead. To taste and season the mixture, if needed.
4. In a big cast iron pan set over medium heat, melt the fat. The seasoned yams or sweet potatoes should be added when oil is shimmering.
5. Stir-fry everything for a minute after tossing it all in the grease. The yams should then simmer for some more minutes with a cover on. When there are some crispy brown parts and the texture is soft & supple, the hash is prepared.
6. You may divide the hash into two halves and top each with a pair of sunny-side-up eggs, or you can serve it with some Aleppo pepper and eat the hash all by yourself. This meal is made substantial and well-rounded with enough protein and fat to go with the carbohydrates, thanks to the inclusion of the eggs, which lend a delicious richness to the hash.
7. A heated 8-inch cast iron pan over medium-low heat should have a tbsp. of ghee added. Two eggs should be cracked into the bowl and carefully poured into the heated pan when the fat begins to sizzle.
8. Based on how gooey you prefer your yolks, season eggs with salt & pepper, and then cover them with the lid for two to three minutes.
9. When they are finished, gently remove them from the pan and place them on top of a pile of hash. Repeat with the other eggs. More Aleppo pepper should be added on top.
10. Per Serving
11. Total Calories: 574kcal, Fats: 31g, Carbohydrates: 60g, Protein: 14g, Fiber: 9g, Sodium: 150mg, Potassium: 90mg

Vegan Avocado Caesar Mix

Prep time: 20 minutes | Cook time: 10 minutes | Serves 4

Vegan Caesar Dressing
- 1 cup of vegan mayo
- 1 tablespoon of Dijon mustard
- 1 tablespoon of briny green peppercorns, drained
- 1½ teaspoons of capers, drained
- 2 roasted garlic cloves
- Cashew Parmesan
- ⅔ cup of nutritional yeast
- 1 tablespoon of salt
- 1⅓ cups of roasted cashews, unsalted
- Vegetable Mix
- 2 cups of mixed greens
- ¼ cup of cashew Parmesan
- 2 romaine lettuce, large heads, whole leaves
- 2 avocados
- Half cup of vegan Caesar dressing

1. In a bowl, add the dressing ingredients. Blend with a stick blender until smooth.
2. In a food processor, add the cashew parmesan ingredients, pulse until smooth.
3. In a bowl, add vegetable mixture and add dressing and cashew mixture (do not add all the cashew mix or all the dressing, use as per taste).
4. Toss and serve with the main course.

PER SERVING

Calories: 315 Total fat: 23 g Total carbs: 28 g Fiber: 7 g Sugar: 6 g Protein: 9 g Sodium: 201 mg

Cinnamon Maple Glazed Carrots

Prep time: 10 minutes | Cook time: 15 minutes | Serves 4

- 1 lb. of small mixed colored carrots
- Sea salt, to taste
- Half cup of water
- 1 teaspoon of ground cinnamon
- 1 teaspoon of coconut oil
- 1 to 2 tablespoons of maple syrup

1. In a pot, sauté carrots in hot oil for 2 minutes.
2. Add water and simmer, partially covered, for ten minutes.
3. As the water is almost evaporated, add rest of the ingredients, mix well.
4. Serve.

PER SERVING

Calories: 63 Total fat: 1 g Total carbs: 13 g Fiber: 3 g Sugar: 8 g Protein: 0 g Sodium: 299 mg

Red Cabbage Mexican Slaw

Prep time: 15 minutes| Cook time: 0 minutes| Serves 8

- 3 cups of shredded Red cabbage
- Half cup of Pomegranate arils
- 4 shredded carrots
- 3 cups of shredded white cabbage
- 1/3 cup of chopped cashews
- 1 cup lime juice
- ¾ cup of chopped fresh cilantro
- 1/4 cup of oil mayonnaise
- 1 teaspoon of red chili flakes

1. In a bowl, toss the carrots and cabbage. Add lime juice and toss.
2. Add rest of the ingredients, mix and serve.

PER SERVING

Calories: 122 Total fat: 8 g Total carbs: 11 g Fiber: 3 g Sugar: 5 g Protein: 2 g Sodium: 299 mg

Spinach Artichoke Twice Baked Potatoes

Prep time: 15 minutes| Cook time: 90 minutes| Serves 4-8

- 5 ounces of baby spinach, fresh
- Half diced onion
- 4 russet potatoes
- 2 minced garlic cloves
- 5.3 ounces of canned coconut cream
- 2 tablespoon of coconut oil
- 1.5 Tablespoon of lemon juice
- 3/4 teaspoon of sea salt
- 2 tablespoon of nutritional yeast

1. Coat the potatoes in oil and season with salt, bake for 60 minutes at 400 F.
2. Slice the potatoes in half and take the middle part out, leave a layer.
3. In a skillet, heat oil on medium flame and sauté onion until translucent, add garlic and cook for 1 minute.
4. Add spinach and cook until wilted.
5. Add artichokes and cook for 1 minutes, season to taste. Turn the heat off.
6. In a bowl, add potato's inside of only three potatoes with salt, coconut oil, lemon juice and nutritional yeast. Mash and mix with artichoke mixture and stuff the potatoes skin.
7. Bake for 15 to 20 minutes at 400 F.
8. Serve.

PER SERVING

Calories: 322 Total fat: 6.9 g Total carbs: 12 g Fiber: 3.2 g Sugar: 3.9 g Protein: 2 g Sodium: 191 mg

Sweet Potato Pegan Bowl

Prep time: 5 minutes | Cook time: 0 minutes | Serves 1

Some sliced pear
- 1 skin-on sweet potato, microwaved or baked till soft inside
- Some almond butter, pepitas, almond yogurt, dried cherries, hemp hearts, dried cranberries, cacao nibs

1. Add all of your preferred toppings to the dish with the cooked sweet potato.

PER SERVING

Total Calories: 112kcal, Fats: 1g, Carbohydrates: 26g, Protein: 2g, Fiber: 4g, Sodium: 72mg, Potassium: 438mg

Cauliflower Gnocchi

Prep time: 20 minutes | Cook time: 40 minutes | Serves 4

Gnocchi:
- 3/4 cup of cassava flour
- 4 cups of cauliflower minced
- 1/2 tsp. of sea salt optional
- Sauce:
- 4 cups of spinach
- 1 can of full-fat coconut milk, canned
- 2 garlic cloves (large)
- salt & pepper to taste
- 2 tbsp. of tapioca flour

1. Heat the oven to 425F.
2. For approximately five minutes, steam the cauliflower until it's tender. Put the cauliflower into a dish towel and squeeze the extra water out to remove the water. About 1 1/2 cups of the leftover cauliflower should be measured.
3. Blend the gnocchi ingredients into a food processor until they are smooth.
4. Roll out the dough in four equal pieces and divide it into "on a board lightly dusted with cassava flour, diameter tubes. Cut the dough tubes into 1 "pieces.
5. Gnocchi is added to boiling water in a big saucepan. Remove them after they have reached the top and spritz with a little olive oil.
6. Gnocchi should be placed on a baking sheet covered with parchment paper & gently greased. After 20 minutes of baking at 425°F, flip the gnocchi over & bake for a further 20 minutes, or until golden.
7. Except for the spinach, combine all of the sauce's components in a saucepan and whisk constantly until the mixture is smooth & the sauce starts to thicken. The flour will make it overly thick and sticky if you overcook it. Keep stirring to prevent clumps. Then turn the heat off, add the spinach, let it wilt, and toss in the gnocchi.

PER SERVING

Total Calories: 298kcal, Fats: 14g, Carbohydrates: 39g, Protein: 7g, Fiber: 8g, Sodium: 129mg, Potassium: 1062mg

Egg Filled Avocado

Prep time:10 minutes | Cook time:22 minutes | Serves 4

- 2 medium avocados, halved and pitted
- 4 small organic eggs
- 6 cherry tomatoes, sliced
- ¼ cup fresh basil leaves, chopped
- Salt and freshly ground black pepper, to taste

1. Preheat the oven to 450 degrees F.
2. Lightly grease a baking dish.
3. Scoop out some flesh from each avocado half to create a cup.
4. Arrange avocado halves, cut side up in prepared baking dish.
5. Carefully, crack each egg into each avocado half.
6. Divide tomato slices over eggs evenly.
7. Bake for about 20-22 minutes.
8. Sprinkle with salt, and black pepper.
9. Garnish with basil and Serve.

PER SERVING

Calories: 239Fat: 19.5gSodium: 63mg Carbohydrates: 12gFiber: 6.9g Sugar: 3.9g
Protein: 7.3g

Frijoles De La Olla

Prep time: 15minutes | Cook time: 65minutes | Serves 4

- 1-pound dry pinto beans, rinsed
- 1 small yellow onion, diced
- 1 jalapeño pepper, seeded and finely chopped
- 1.1/2 teaspoons minced garlic (3 cloves)
- 1 tablespoon ground cumin
- 1/2 teaspoon Mexican oregano (optional)
- 1 teaspoon red pepper flakes (optional)
- 4 cups water
- 2 tablespoons salt

1. Place the beans, onion, jalapeño, garlic, cumin, oregano (if using), red pepper flakes (if using), water, and salt in a slow cooker.
2. Cook on low heat.

PER SERVING

Calories: 256 Total fat: 8g Protein: 28g

Balsamic Mushrooms

Prep time: 30 minutes| Cook time: 20 minutes| Serves 4

- 2 tablespoons of balsamic vinegar
- 1 lb. of mushrooms
- Half teaspoon of dried parsley
- 2 tablespoons of olive oil
- 1 teaspoon of minced garlic minced
- 1/4 teaspoon of pepper
- Half teaspoon of dried basil
- Half teaspoon of salt

1. In a bowl, add all ingredients, except for mushrooms.
2. Mix and add mushrooms, let it rest for 20 minutes.
3. Spread on a foil lined baking sheet and roast for 20 minutes at 400 F.

PER SERVING

Calories: 96 Total fat: 7 g Total carbs: 5 g Fiber: 1 g Sugar: 3 g Protein: 4 g Sodium: 299 mg

Broccoli Casserole

Prep Time: 10 minutes | Cook time: 45 minutes | Serves 6

- 1/3 cup of heavy whipping cream
- 3 whisked eggs
- 1/2 cup of grated parmesan cheese
- Some pepper, to taste
- 1 tsp. of sea salt
- 6 cups of cauliflower rice
- 4 cups of broccoli florets
- 2 packages of smoked canadian bacon
- 2 cups of cheddar cheese

1. Set the oven to 425°F.
2. Combine the eggs, parmesan, heavy whipping cream, cheese, salt, and pepper in a medium mixing bowl.
3. Cauliflower rice, broccoli, ham, and the egg mixture should all be placed in a 9-by-9-inch casserole dish. Mix the items together with a fork.
4. Cheddar cheese shreds should be placed on top of the dish.
5. Bake the casserole for 35 minutes with the foil covering. To give the cheese brown color on top, uncover the dish and bake it for an additional 10 minutes.

PER SERVING

Total Calories: 431kcal, Fat: 26g, Carbohydrates: 18g, Protein: 33g, Fiber: 6g, Sodium: 1396mg, Potassium: 1189mg

Pumpkin Chili

Prep time: 10 minutes | Cook time: 30 minutes | Serves 8

- 1/2 lb. of beef or ground pork (organic), if preferred
- 1 lb. of ground beef, grass-fed
- Sea salt & black pepper
- 1 onion (medium), diced
- 1/2 tbsp. of olive oil or avocado oil for browning of the meat
- 1 green bell pepper (large), diced
- 1 minced jalapeno pepper
- 4 cloves of garlic minced
- 3/4 - 1 tsp. of sea salt, adjust it to taste
- 1 can of diced tomatoes (14.5 oz.), no salt added & not drained
- 1 can of crushed tomatoes (28 oz.)
- 1 can of pumpkin puree (15 oz.)
- 3/4 tsp. of smoked paprika
- 2 tsp. of chili powder
- 1/4 tsp. of chipotle powder
- 1 1/2 tsp. of cinnamon or pumpkin spice, if preferred
- 1 tsp. of cumin
- Chopped cilantro (fresh) for garnish

1. Coconut oil is added to a Dutch oven that is already hot to the touch. Use a spoon or fork to break up lumps as the meat and pork are added, then season with sea salt & black pepper and brown evenly.
2. When it is halfway done, add the onions & peppers and, if desired, drain some of the fat (but not all). Stir and heat for another 2 minutes, or until the meat is browned and the pepper and onions are beginning to soften. No further fat should be drained. Stir in the garlic and jalapeno, then simmer for an additional minute.
3. Reduce the heat before adding the pumpkin, diced tomatoes, crushed tomatoes, 1/2 teaspoon salt, and all the spices. Stir well, then turn up the heat to bring it to a boil. As soon as it begins to bubble, reduce heat to a moderate simmer, cover, and let the mixture simmer for 15 minutes at least (and as long as 45) to blend the flavors. This chili is excellent as leftovers since the taste just gets stronger as it simmers.
4. To serve, garnish with cilantro, diced avocado, red onion, and sour cream. For up to 4 days, keep leftovers sealed in the refrigerator.

PER SERVING

Total Calories: 218kcal, Fats: 15g, Carbohydrates: 3g, Protein: 15g, Fiber: 1g, Sodium: 211mg, Potassium: 313mg

Nachos

Prep time: 5 minutes | Cook time:10 minutes | Serves 4

- 4-ounce restaurant-style tortilla corn chips
- 1 medium green onion, thinly sliced (about 1 tbsp.)
- 1 (4 ounces) package finely crumbled feta cheese
- 1 finely chopped and drained plum tomato
- 2 tbsp. Sun-dried tomatoes in oil, finely chopped
- 2 tbsp. Kalamata olives

1. Mix the onion, plum tomato, oil, sun-dried tomatoes, and olives in a small bowl.
2. Arrange the tortillas chips on a microwavable plate in a single layer topped evenly with cheese—microwave on high for one minute.
3. Rotate the plate half turn and continue microwaving until the cheese is bubbly. Spread the tomato mixture over the chips and cheese and enjoy.

PER SERVING

Calories: 140 Carbs: 19g Fat: 7g Protein: 2g

Stuffed Celery

Prep time: 15 minutes | Cook time:20 minutes | Serves 3

- Olive oil
- 1 clove garlic, minced
- 2 tbsp. pine nuts
- 2 tbsps. dry-roasted sunflower seeds
- ¼ cup Italian cheese blend, shredded
- 8 stalks celery leaves
- 1 (8-ounce) fat-free cream cheese
- Cooking spray

1. Sauté garlic and pine nuts in one tablespoon oil over a medium heat until the nuts are golden brown. Cut off the wide base and tops from celery.
2. Remove two thin strips from the round side of the celery to create a flat surface.
3. Mix Italian cheese and cream cheese in a bowl and spread into cut celery stalks.
4. Sprinkle half of the celery pieces with sunflower seeds and a half with the pine nut mixture. Cover mixture and let stand for at least 4 hours before eating.

PER SERVING

Calories: 64 Carbs: 2g Fat: 6g Protein: 1g

Butternut Squash Fries

Prep time: 5 minutes | Cook time:10 minutes | Serves 2

- 1 butternut squash
- 1 tbsp. Extra virgin olive oil
- ½ tbsp. grapeseed oil
- 1/8 tsp. sea salt

1. Remove seeds from the squash and cut into thin slices. Coat with extra virgin olive oil and grapeseed oil. Add a sprinkle of salt and toss to coat well.
2. Arrange the squash slices onto three oiled baking sheets and bake for 10 minutes until crispy.

PER SERVING

Calories: 40 Carbs: 10g Fat: 0g Protein: 1g

Dried Fig Tapenade

Prep time: 5 minutes | Cook time:0 minutes | Serves 1

- 1 cup dried figs
- 1 cup Kalamata olives
- ½ cup water
- 1 tbsp. chopped fresh thyme
- 1 tbsp. extra virgin olive oil
- ½ tsp. balsamic vinegar

1. Prepare figs in a food processor until well chopped, add water, and continue processing to form a paste.
2. Add olives and pulse until well blended.
3. Add thyme, vinegar, and extra virgin olive oil and pulse until very smooth. Best served with crackers of your choice.

PER SERVING

Calories: 249 Carbs: 64g Fat: 1g Protein: 3g

Speedy Sweet Potato Chips

Prep time: 15 minutes | Cook time:0 minutes | Serves 4

- 1 large Sweet potato
- 1 tbsp. Extra virgin olive oil
- Salt

1. 300°F preheated oven. Slice your potato into nice, thin slices that resemble fries.
2. Toss the potato slices with salt and extra virgin olive oil in a bowl. Bake for about one hour, flipping every 15 minutes until crispy and browned.

PER SERVING

Calories: 150 Carbs: 16g Fat: 9g Protein: 1g

Nachos with Hummus (Mediterranean Inspired)

Prep time: 15 minutes | Cook time:20 minutes | Serves 4

- 4 cups salted pita chips
- 1 (8 oz.) red pepper (roasted)
- 1 cup hummus
- 1 tsp. Finely shredded lemon peel
- ¼ cup Chopped pitted Kalamata olives
- ¼ cup crumbled feta cheese
- 1 plum (Roma) tomato, seeded, chopped
- ½ cup chopped cucumber
- 1 tsp. Chopped fresh oregano leaves

1. 400°F preheated oven. Arrange the pita chips on a baking sheet and cover with hummus.
2. Top with olives, tomato, cucumber, and cheese and bake until warmed through. Sprinkle lemon zest and oregano and enjoy while it's hot.

PER SERVING

Calories: 130 Carbs: 18g Fat: 5g Protein: 4g

Hummus and Olive Pita Bread

Prep time: 5 minutes | Cook time:0 minutes | Serves 3

- 7 pita bread cut into 6 wedges each
- 1 (7 ounces) container plain hummus
- 1 tbsp. Greek vinaigrette
- ½ cup Chopped pitted Kalamata olives

1. Spread the hummus on a serving plate—Mix vinaigrette and olives in a bowl and spoon over the hummus. Enjoy with wedges of pita bread.

PER SERVING

Calories: 225 Carbs: 40g Fat: 5g Protein: 9g

Roast Asparagus

Prep time: 15 minutes | Cook time:5 minutes | Serves 4

- 1 tbsp. Extra virgin olive oil (1 tablespoon)
- 1 medium lemon
- ½ tsp. Freshly grated nutmeg
- ½ tsp. black pepper
- ½ tsp. Kosher salt

1. Warm the oven to 500°F. Put the asparagus on an aluminum foil and drizzle with extra virgin olive oil, and toss until well coated.
2. Roast the asparagus in the oven for about five minutes; toss and continue roasting until browned. Sprinkle the roasted asparagus with nutmeg, salt, zest, and pepper.

PER SERVING

Calories: 123 Carbs: 5g Fat: 11g Protein: 3g

Summertime Vegetable Chicken Wraps

Prep time: 15 minutes | Cook time:0 minutes | Serves 4

- 2 cups cooked chicken, chopped
- ½ English cucumbers, diced
- ½ red bell pepper, diced
- ½ cup carrot, shredded
- 1 scallion, white and green parts, chopped
- ¼ cup plain Greek yogurt
- 1 tablespoon freshly squeezed lemon juice
- ½ teaspoon fresh thyme, chopped
- Pinch of salt
- Pinch of ground black pepper
- 4 multigrain tortillas

1. Take a medium bowl and mix in chicken, red bell pepper, cucumber, carrot, yogurt, scallion, lemon juice, thyme, sea salt and pepper.
2. Mix well.
3. Spoon one quarter of chicken mix into the middle of the tortilla and fold the opposite ends of the tortilla over the filling.
4. Roll the tortilla from the side to create a snug pocket.
5. Repeat with the remaining ingredients and serve.
6. Enjoy!

PER SERVING

Calories: 278 Fat: 4g Carbohydrates: 28g Protein: 27g

Premium Roasted Baby Potatoes

Prep time: 10 minutes | Cook time:35 minutes | Serves 4

- 2 pounds new yellow potatoes, scrubbed and cut into wedges
- 2 tablespoons extra virgin olive oil
- 2 teaspoons fresh rosemary, chopped
- 1 teaspoon garlic powder
- 1 teaspoon sweet paprika
- ½ teaspoon sea salt
- ½ teaspoon freshly ground black pepper

1. Pre-heat your oven to 400 degrees Fahrenheit.
2. Take a large bowl and add potatoes, olive oil, garlic, rosemary, paprika, sea salt and pepper.
3. Spread potatoes in single layer on baking sheet and bake for 35 minutes.
4. Serve and enjoy!

PER SERVING

Calories: 225 Fat: 7g Carbohydrates: 37g Protein: 5g

Zaatar Fries

Prep time: 10 minutes | Cook time:35 minutes | Serves 5

- 1 teaspoon Za'atar spices
- 3 sweet potatoes
- 1 tablespoon dried dill
- 1 teaspoon salt
- 3 teaspoons sunflower oil
- ½ teaspoon paprika

1. Cut the sweet potatoes into fries.
2. Line the baking tray with parchment paper. Layer of the sweet potato in the tray.
3. Sprinkle the vegetables with dried dill, salt, and paprika. Then sprinkle sweet potatoes with Za'atar and mix well...
4. Sprinkle the sweet potato fries with sunflower oil—preheat the oven to 375F.
5. Bake the sweet potato fries within 35 minutes. Stir the fries every 10 minutes.

PER SERVING

Calories 28 Fat 2.9 Fiber 0.2 Carbs 0.6 Protein 0.2

Chapter 14
Snack & Dessert

Nacho Cheese
Prep time: 10 minutes | Cook time: 15 minutes| Serves 4

- 2 cups peeled chopped russet potatoes
- 1 cup chopped carrots
- 1/2 to 3/4 cup water
- 1 tablespoon freshly squeezed lemon juice
- 1/2 cup nutritional yeast
- 1/2 teaspoon onion powder
- 1/2 teaspoon garlic powder
- 1 teaspoon salt
- 1/4 cup salsa store bought (optional)

1. Stew the potatoes and carrots until soft, about 15 minutes.
2. Put 1/2 cup of water into a blender, followed by the lemon juice, nutritional yeast, onion powder, garli powder, salt, and salsa (if using).
3. Blend until completely smooth. If the consistency is too thick, add the remaining 1/4 cup of water to thin it out.

PER SERVING

Calories: 237 Fat: 1g Protein: 13g Sodium: 724mg Fiber: 11g

Mushroom Gravy
Prep time: 10 minutes | Cook time: 10 minutes| Serves 4

- 1 tablespoon oil
- 1 small yellow onion, diced
- 1 cup finely chopped button mushrooms
- 11/2 teaspoons minced garlic (3 cloves)
- 4 tablespoons flour
- 11/4 cups water
- 1 tablespoon soy sauce
- 1/2 teaspoon dried oregano
- 2 bay leaves
- Freshly ground black pepper

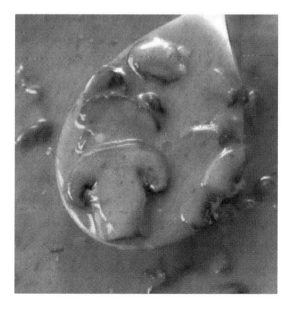

1. Warmth the oil in a saucepan, then attach the onion, mushrooms, and garlic. Sauté until the onions are translucent.
2. Attach the flour and mix to form a thick paste.
3. Add the water, soy sauce, oregano, and bay leaves, and bring to a simmer over medium heat. Season with pepper.
4. Remove the bay leaves. Use a whisk to gently merge the gravy until it thickens. Add more water if you prefer thinner gravy.

PER SERVING

Calories: 79 Fat: 4g Protein: 2g Sodium: 230mg Fiber: 1g

The Greatest Guacamole
Prep time: 10 minutes | Cook time: 0 minutes| Serves 4

- 2 large avocados, halved, peeled, and roughly chopped
- Juice of 1/2 lime
- 2 teaspoons olive oil
- 1/4 red onion, finely diced
- 1/2 teaspoon minced garlic (1 clove)
- 1/2 teaspoon ground cumin
- 1 tablespoon freshly chopped cilantro
- 1/2 Roma tomato, diced
- Pinch salt
- Freshly ground black pepper

1. Mash the avocados to the desired consistency in a medium-size bowl.
2. Add the lime juice and oil. Stir in the red onion, garlic, cumin, cilantro, and tomato, then season with salt and pepper.

PER SERVING

Calories: 233 Fat: 22g Protein: 2g Sodium: 48mg Fiber: 7g

Super Simple Salsa
Prep time: 10 minutes | Cook time: 0 minutes| Serves 4

- 2 cups chopped tomatoes
- 1/2 cup diced yellow onion
- 2 tablespoons minced cilantro
- Juice of 1/2 lime, plus more for seasoning (optional)
- 1 jalapeño pepper, seeded and chopped
- 1/2 teaspoon ground cumin
- Pinch salt
- Freshly ground black pepper

1. Combine the tomatoes, onion, cilantro, lime juice, jalapeño, and cumin in a bowl; mix well.
2. Flavor with salt and pepper, and add more lime juice (if using).

PER SERVING

Calories: 25 Fat: 1g Protein: 1g Sodium: 46mg Fiber: 2g

Cashew Cream

Prep time: 5 minutes | Cook time: 0 minutes | Serves 4

- 1 cup raw cashews,
- 1/2 cup water
- 1/4 teaspoon salt
- Freshly ground black pepper

1. Place the soaked cashews, water, and salt in a high-speed blender or food processor; blend until completely smooth.
2. Season with pepper.

PER SERVING

Calories: 197 Fat: 16g Protein: 5g Sodium: 154mg Fiber: 1g

Spinach Dip

Prep time: 20 minutes | Cook time: 5 minutes | Serves 8

- ¾ cup cashews
- 3.5 ounces' soft tofu
- 6 ounces of spinach leaves
- 1 medium white onion, peeled, diced
- 2 teaspoons minced garlic
- ½ teaspoon salt
- 3 tablespoons olive oil

1. Place cashews in a bowl, cover with hot water, and then let them soak for 15 minutes.
2. After 15 minutes, drain the cashews and then set aside until required.
3. Take a medium skillet pan, add oil to it and then place the pan over medium heat.
4. Add onion, cook for 3 to 5 minutes until tender, stir in garlic and then continue cooking for 30 seconds until fragrant.
5. Spoon the onion mixture into a blender, add remaining ingredients and then pulse until smooth.
6. Tip the dip into a bowl and then serve with chips.

PER SERVING

Calories: 134.6 Cal;Fat: 8.6 g; Protein: 10 g; Carbs: 6.3 g; Fiber: 1.4 g

Tomatillo Salsa

Prep time: 5 minutes | Cook time: 15 minutes | Serves 8

- 5 medium tomatillos, chopped
- 3 cloves of garlic, peeled, chopped
- 3 Roma tomatoes, chopped
- 1 jalapeno, chopped
- ½ of a medium red onion, peeled, chopped
- 1 Anaheim chili
- 2 teaspoons salt
- 1 teaspoon ground cumin
- 1 lime, juiced
- ¼ cup cilantro leaves
- ¾ cup of water

1. Take a medium pot, place it over medium heat, pour in water, and then add onion, tomatoes, tomatillo, jalapeno, and Anaheim chili.
2. Sauté the vegetables for 15 minutes, remove the pot from heat, add cilantro and lime juice and then stir in salt.
3. Remove pot from heat and then pulse by using an immersion blender until smooth.
4. Serve the salsa with chips.

PER SERVING

Calories: 317.4 Cal; Fat: 0 g; Protein: 16 g; Carbs: 64 g; Fiber: 16 g

Arugula Pesto Couscous

Prep time: 10 minutes | Cook time: 20 minutes | Serves 4

- 8 ounces' Israeli couscous
- 3 large tomatoes, chopped
- 3 cups arugula leaves
- ½ cup parsley leaves
- 6 cloves of garlic, peeled
- ½ cup walnuts
- ¾ teaspoon salt
- 1 cup and 1 tablespoon olive oil
- 2 cups vegetable broth

1. Take a medium saucepan, place it over medium-high heat, add 1 tablespoon oil and then let it heat.
2. Add couscous, stir until mixed, and then cook for 4 minutes until fragrant and toasted.
3. Pour in the broth, stir until mixed, bring it to a boil, switch heat to medium level and then simmer for 12 minutes until the couscous has absorbed all the liquid and turn tender.
4. When done, remove the pan from heat, fluff it with a fork, and then set aside until required.
5. While couscous cooks, prepare the pesto, and for this, place walnuts in a blender, add garlic, and then pulse until nuts have broken.
6. Add arugula, parsley, and salt, pulse until well combined, and then blend in oil until smooth.
7. Transfer couscous to a salad bowl, add tomatoes and prepared pesto, and then toss until mixed.
8. Serve straight away.

PER SERVING

Calories: 73 Cal; Fat: 4 g; Protein: 2 g; Carbs: 8 g; Fiber: 2 g

Pico de Gallo

Prep time: 5 minutes| Cook time: 0 minutes| Serves 6

- ½ of a medium red onion, peeled, chopped
- 2 cups diced tomato
- ½ cup chopped cilantro
- 1 jalapeno pepper, minced
- 1/8 teaspoon salt
- ¼ teaspoon ground black pepper
- ½ of a lime, juiced
- 1 teaspoon olive oil

1. Take a large bowl, place all the ingredients in it and then stir until well mixed.
2. Serve the Pico de Gallo with chips.

PER SERVING

Calories: 790 Cal; Fat: 6.4 g; Protein: 25.6 g; Carbs: 195.2 g; Fiber: 35.2 g

Blueberry Pancakes

Prep time:5 minutes | Cook time:10 minutes | Serves 4

- ½ cup coconut flour
- 1 teaspoon baking soda
- 2 drops liquid stevia
- Pinch of salt
- 4 organic eggs
- 1 cup unsweetened almond milk
- 1 teaspoon organic vanilla extract
- 2 tablespoons fresh blueberries
- 2 tablespoons coconut oil
- 2 tablespoons maple syrup

1. In a large bowl, mix together flour, baking soda and salt.
2. In another bowl, add egg, milk and vanilla extract and beat till well combined.
3. Add egg mixture into flour mixture and mix till well combined.
4. Gently, fold in blueberries.
5. In a large skillet, heat oil on medium heat.
6. Add desired amount of mixture in the skillet. With the back of wooden spoon, spread the mixture in skillet evenly.
7. Cook for about 2-3 minutes. Carefully, change the side and cook for 1-2 minutes further.
8. Repeat with remaining mixture.
9. Serve with the drizzling of maple syrup.

PER SERVING

Calories: 233Fat: 14.6gSodium: 491mg Carbohydrates: 17.3gFiber: 6.4g Sugar: 7.9g
Protein: 8.8g

Beet Balls

Prep time: 10 minutes| Cook time: 0 minutes| Serves 6

- ½ cup oats
- 1 medium beet, cooked
- ½ cup almond flour
- 1/3 cup shredded coconut and more for coating
- ¾ cup Medjool dates, pitted
- 1 tablespoon cocoa powder
- ¼ cup chocolate chips, unsweetened

1. Place cooked beets in a blender and then pulse until chopped into very small pieces.
2. Add remaining ingredients and then pulse until the dough comes together.
3. Shape the dough into eighteen balls, coat them in some more coconut and then serve.

PER SERVING

Calories: 114.2 Cal; Fat: 2.4 g; Protein: 5 g; Carbs: 19.6 g; Fiber: 4.9 g

Cheesy Crackers

Prep time: 10 minutes| Cook time: 20 minutes| Serves 3

- 1 ¾ cup almond meal
- 3 tablespoons nutritional yeast
- ½ teaspoon of sea salt
- 2 tablespoons lemon juice
- 1 tablespoon melted coconut oil
- 1 tablespoon ground flaxseed
- 2 ½ tablespoons water

1. Switch on the oven, then set it to 350 degrees F and let it preheat.
2. Meanwhile, take a medium bowl, place flaxseed in it, stir in water, and then let the mixture rest for 5 minutes until thickened.
3. Place almond meal in a medium bowl, add salt and yeast and then stir until mixed.
4. Add lemon juice and oil into the flaxseed mixture and then whisk until mixed.
5. Pour the flaxseed mixture into the almond meal mixture and then stir until dough comes together.
6. Place a piece of a wax paper on a clean working space, place the dough on it, cover with another piece of wax paper, and then roll dough into a 1/8-inch-thick crust.
7. Cut the dough into a square shape, sprinkle salt over the top and then bake for 15 to 20 minutes until done. Serve straight away.

PER SERVING

Calories: 30 Cal; Fat: 1 g; Protein: 1 g; Carbs: 5 g; Fiber: 0 g

Chia Seed Pudding

Prep time: 15 minutes | **Cook time:** 0 minutes | **Serves 2**

- 1 cup unsweetened almond milk
- 2 tablespoons maple syrup
- ¼ cup chia seeds
- ¼ teaspoon organic vanilla extract
- ½ of small apple, cored and sliced
- 2 tablespoons almonds, chopped

1. In a large bowl, add all ingredients except apple and almonds and stir to combine well.
2. Cover and refrigerate for at least 30-40 minutes.
3. Top with apple and almonds and serve.

PER SERVING

Calories: 185 Fat: 9.8g Sodium: 92mg Carbohydrates: 26.9g Fiber: 7.1g Sugar: 16.1g Protein: 4.9g

Meatballs Platter

Prep time: 10 minutes | **Cook time:** 15 minutes | **Serves 4**

- 1-pound beef meat, ground
- ¼ cup panko bread crumbs
- A pinch of salt and black pepper
- 3 tablespoons red onion, grated
- ¼ cup parsley, chopped
- 2 garlic cloves, minced
- 2 tablespoons lemon juice
- Zest of 1 lemon, grated
- 1 egg
- ½ teaspoon cumin, ground
- ½ teaspoon coriander, ground
- ¼ teaspoon cinnamon powder
- 2 ounces' feta cheese, crumbled
- Cooking spray

1. In a bowl, blend the beef with the breadcrumbs, salt, pepper and the rest of the ingredients except the cooking spray, stir well and shape medium balls out of this mix.
2. Arrange the meatballs on a baking sheet lined with parchment paper, grease them with cooking spray and bake at 450 degrees F for 15 minutes.
3. Position the meatballs on a platter and serve as a snack.

PER SERVING

Calories: 300, Fat: 15.4, Fiber: 6.4, Carbs: 22.4, Protein: 35

Yogurt Dip

Prep time: 10 minutes | **Cook time:** 0 minutes | **Serves 6**

- 2 cups Greek yogurt
- 2 tablespoons pistachios, toasted and chopped
- A pinch of salt and white pepper
- 2 tablespoons mint, chopped
- 1 tablespoon kalamata olives, pitted and chopped
- ¼ cup za'atar spice
- ¼ cup pomegranate seeds
- 1/3 cup olive oil

1. In a bowl, blend the yogurt with the pistachios and the rest of the ingredients, whisk well.
2. Divide into small cups and serve with pita chips on the side.

PER SERVING

Calories: 294, Fat: 18, Fiber: 1, Carbs: 21, Protein: 10

Appendix 1 Measurement Conversion Chart

Volume Equivalents (Dry)

US STANDARD	METRIC (APPROXIMATE)
1/8 teaspoon	0.5 mL
1/4 teaspoon	1 mL
1/2 teaspoon	2 mL
3/4 teaspoon	4 mL
1 teaspoon	5 mL
1 tablespoon	15 mL
1/4 cup	59 mL
1/2 cup	118 mL
3/4 cup	177 mL
1 cup	235 mL
2 cups	475 mL
3 cups	700 mL
4 cups	1 L

Volume Equivalents (Liquid)

US STANDARD	US STANDARD (OUNCES)	METRIC (APPROXIMATE)
2 tablespoons	1 fl.oz.	30 mL
1/4 cup	2 fl.oz.	60 mL
1/2 cup	4 fl.oz.	120 mL
1 cup	8 fl.oz.	240 mL
1 1/2 cup	12 fl.oz.	355 mL
2 cups or 1 pint	16 fl.oz.	475 mL
4 cups or 1 quart	32 fl.oz.	1 L
1 gallon	128 fl.oz.	4 L

Temperatures Equivalents

FAHRENHEIT(F)	CELSIUS(C) APPROXIMATE
225 °F	107 °C
250 °F	120 ° °C
275 °F	135 °C
300 °F	150 °C
325 °F	160 °C
350 °F	180 °C
375 °F	190 °C
400 °F	205 °C
425 °F	220 °C
450 °F	235 °C
475 °F	245 °C
500 °F	260 °C

Weight Equivalents

US STANDARD	METRIC (APPROXIMATE)
1 ounce	28 g
2 ounces	57 g
5 ounces	142 g
10 ounces	284 g
15 ounces	425 g
16 ounces (1 pound)	455 g
1.5 pounds	680 g
2 pounds	907 g

Appendix 2 The Dirty Dozen and Clean Fifteen

The Environmental Working Group (EWG) is a nonprofit, nonpartisan organization dedicated to protecting human health and the environment Its mission is to empower people to live healthier lives in a healthier environment. This organization publishes an annual list of the twelve kinds of produce, in sequence, that have the highest amount of pesticide residue-the Dirty Dozen-as well as a list of the fifteen kinds ofproduce that have the least amount of pesticide residue-the Clean Fifteen.

THE DIRTY DOZEN	
The 2016 Dirty Dozen includes the following produce. These are considered among the year's most important produce to buy organic:	
Strawberries	Spinach
Apples	Tomatoes
Nectarines	Bell peppers
Peaches	Cherry tomatoes
Celery	Cucumbers
Grapes	Kale/collard greens
Cherries	Hot peppers
The Dirty Dozen list contains two additional itemskale/ collard greens and hot peppers-because they tend to contain trace levels of highly hazardous pesticides.	

THE CLEAN FIFTEEN	
The least critical to buy organically are the Clean Fifteen list. The following are on the 2016 list:	
Avocados	Papayas
Corn	Kiw
Pineapples	Eggplant
Cabbage	Honeydew
Sweet peas	Grapefruit
Onions	Cantaloupe
Asparagus	Cauliflower
Mangos	
Some of the sweet corn sold in the United States are made from genetically engineered (GE) seedstock. Buy organic varieties of these crops to avoid GE produce.	

Appendix 3: Index

W

Z

ALANA J. EILERS

Made in the USA
Las Vegas, NV
28 January 2023

66383507R00068